WHAT THEY DON'T TEACH IN ART SCHOOL

You can find more book like this at:
wellfedillustrators.com

WHAT THEY DON'T TEACH IN ART SCHOOL

WILL TERRY

An illustrator's guide to making money in the real world

Text copyright © 2020 by Will Terry.
Cover art and illustration art copyright © 2020 by Will Terry.

All rights reserved. No part of this book may be reproduced in any form without permission from the author/publisher. Published in the United States by Giggledesk, in association with Well Fed Illustrators LLC in Orem, Utah, in 2020. Visit us on the web at **www.wellfedillustrators.com**

All editing by Kim MacPherson.
Book Designed by Maralee Nelson / mGraphicDesign.

ISBN: 978-0-578-75189-4 / Soft Cover
ISBN: 978-0-578-76422-1 / Hard Cover

The artwork in this book is a collection of both traditionally and digitally created art. Traditional work was created with acrylic paint on 140lb hot press paper and the digital work was drawn on iPad Pro using the Procreate app, and painted in Photoshop on a PC desktop and Wacom Cintiq monitor and stylus.
All artwork created by Will Terry except where specifically noted otherwise.

DEDICATION

To all of my
art teachers,
illustration mentors,
illustration peers,
and the students
who have taught me
so much!

TABLE OF CONTENTS

Why I Wrote This Book 11

How to Be Successful in Art School 17

Becoming a Master Artist 35

Getting Freelance Work After Art School 55

Creating Your Own Brand 81

Getting a Full Time Art Job 115

Professional Practices 123

Afterword 157

What is the Biggest Lesson You've Learned
as a Working Professional Artist? 161

Notes 211

"In order to make a thriving career with your art, you need to be able to not only create great art; you need to know how to *market* your art."

WHY I WROTE THIS BOOK

At the time of the publication of this book, I have been a freelance illustrator for twenty-seven years starting in 1992. I have taught at two universities, lectured at many art schools, and taught online for SVSLearn.com. In that time, I have spent a large portion of my time teaching illustration students design, drawing, painting, and how to make children's books.

Each time I taught a class, I would also work theory, business strategies, entrepreneurship, and common-sense people skills into my lectures. At the end of each class, I would often hear things like, *"I've never had another teacher talk to us the way you did,"* or *"This has been the most informative class I've ever taken in art,"* or *"I learned more in your class than in any other class I've had in this program."*

Don't get me wrong—I don't think I have a corner on the information I'm sharing in this book—I just think that most teachers are NOT incentivized to go beyond the course curriculum as defined in the catalog. In other words, "Not my problem." Then there are those teachers who have never had a career in art aside from their teaching position; therefore, they have no practical advice to share.

In order to make a thriving career with your art, you need to be able to not only create great art; you need to know how to *market* your art.

One of these skills without the other isn't enough—you must have both. There are amazing artists out there who could easily make lots of money but aren't getting freelance work because art buyers don't know they exist. Likewise, there are artists with marketing skills and tenacity who lack the portfolio to land gigs. Art schools focus on teaching their students how to make art and mostly leave students to their own devices to figure out how to sell their work.

Schools are not accountable to students who cannot find work in their chosen profession. In fact, most administrators (if asked) will tell you that they do not exist to help you get a job; yet the freshman marketing brochures are filled with photos of graduates working in their new careers.

Sure, you might have an art school that gives lip service by offering seniors a "business class," but it's often taught by a warm body whose main qualifications consisted of the simple fact that it fit into his or her schedule.

WHY I WROTE THIS BOOK

What's worse is often the information given in the business class covers the things you can find in a quick Google search: self-employment taxes, contracts, business licenses, invoices, etc. What's missing is the information that you need to actually garner the jobs and opportunities that give you the "privilege" to pay taxes, create contracts and invoices, etc.

To be clear, some art schools are very good at teaching technique and the craft of making great images—even art. In fact, many of the greatest illustrators went to great art schools, but their graduates almost always had to learn the rest on their own. I am very grateful for the art training I received, but when I finished school I was lost, and scrambled to find the information I was missing.

What's also missing are the entrepreneurial techniques, strategies, behaviors, and networking advice, as well as the need to be constantly looking for new emerging markets and opportunities with the skills they taught you in art school.

I wanted to write this book because I've spent my life helping other artists learn what I've learned—how to lead a very fulfilling life as a freelance illustrator, teacher, mentor, podcaster, YouTuber, and entrepreneur. We only get a few chances to leave our mark in this world and I'm excited to share my experiences as a working artist and teacher.

I've included my artwork because I've always wanted to release an art anthology book like many artists do when they have developed a body of work. I felt that sharing the work I've spent my life creating along with the teaching I've spent my life giving would combine to communicate and enhance the passion I have for both disciplines.

I can't teach without sharing art and I can't create art without using it to teach.

You are an artist. You love to create. You want to be able to make money with your art. This book will help you make the changes necessary and give you the knowledge to earn a living with your art.

WHY I WROTE THIS BOOK

"My advice is to surrender to the process. Let go. Don't try to drive the ship. Allow your teachers to teach. The best artists are usually the best students. The best students have learned to be humble and teachable."

HOW TO BE SUCCESSFUL IN ART SCHOOL

You are an artist

If you have ever woken up in the morning wanting to create something the world has never experienced, you are an artist. If you've ever felt like you needed to create in order to breathe, you are an artist. If you've ever wanted to express your sincere emotions in words, images, music, or sculpture, you are an artist. If you've ever failed to express yourself in your chosen craft and shed tears of frustration—you are an artist.

You can spend periods of your life working for other people—traveling, socializing, taking care of your family, etc.; but you will always hear the call from your spirit to create. You can try to ignore it, but it will always tap you on the shoulder and whisper to you about your unfulfilled desires to *make* something.

I have known many artists who, after realizing how much work they will have to put into their craft, quit and transitioned into another creative field.

I have known many artists who have quit their craft after they realized how much work it was going to take to become a master. Some switched over to another creative discipline, only to quit again when they discovered that it was going to be equally hard to master the second craft. No matter what flavor of art you decide to make—from music to writing, photography, illustration, or gallery work, you will have to *dedicate your life* to mastering your chosen craft.

You wouldn't want it any different! If it were easy to master your chosen craft, it wouldn't require sacrifice. Let's face it: things that do not require sacrifice are generally worthless. There are millions of children who finger paint in elementary school many times each year. How much do their paintings sell for? You *want* it to be hard because you are going to be more committed to your craft than most artists. Most artists won't seek out books like this one to help them improve their minds and their dedication; yet here you are, still reading. You already have an advantage.

Instead of switching to another craft or major, understand that the going is and will always be tough! Sometimes you will shed tears over the frustration of yet another failed painting or drawing. These tears are wonderful because they are a sign that you care! Show me an artist who has never experienced extreme anger or sorrow over their failures and I'll show you an artist who isn't creating good art.

> **The good news is that if you stick with it long enough (assuming that you are constantly yearning and striving to improve), it will get much easier and really fun!**

The good news is that if you stick with it long enough (assuming that you are constantly yearning and striving to improve), it *will* get much easier and really fun! There's nothing like finally being able to execute the vision of an image you had in your mind!

How to be a great art student

You probably decided to go to art school for one of three reasons:

1. You didn't know what major to pick, but art was an easy class in high school so you thought you would have an easy major by going with art.

2. You have always been good in art or at least you've been told you're good by your friends and family (because, perhaps, you have made more art than your friends and family!); so you chose art as your major because you're "good at art."

3. You have always loved making art and you want to learn how you can get good enough to make it your career.

Hopefully you have already figured out that only one of those answers above demonstrates that you have the mindset to improve your artistic abilities. I have taught a lot of kids who picked art because they thought it wouldn't require much of them. I can't recall any of those students going on to earn a living as an artist.

We've all heard the horror stories from med school students having to study 7 days a week and only getting 4–5 hours of sleep a night to wake up and do it all over again. The commitment it takes to become a doctor or surgeon is scary for most of us because most of us aren't willing to sacrifice at this level. Reading and memorizing and reading and reporting and reading and testing and reading some more… plus the fear of failure as the student loans pile up is vomit-inducing to most of us. But, at the end of the day, almost every student who sticks it out and graduates, ends up with a high-paying job.

Art students have no such guarantee. Art students can be at the top of their class and yet there is no job waiting for them at the end of the day. However, the jobs typically do go to the hardest working students who develop unique styles and are able to make intelligent choices with their portfolios and how they market their work. So, the art students who take art because it's an easy major are just wasting four years of tuition. If anything, art students should be working HARDER than med students because it's more difficult for art students to develop a career with their art.

If you thought #2 was a good reason, it's not. If you're already good at art, why are you paying for art school? Why aren't you making lots of money with your art skills? I'm going to ask you to really think about this—where do you fit in the food chain of amateur, novice, semi-pro, and professional artists?

HOW TO BE SUCCESSFUL IN ART SCHOOL

The art students who take art because it's an easy major are just wasting four years of tuition. If anything, art students should be working HARDER than med students because it's more difficult for art students to develop a career with their art.

I have taught many art students who thought they already had a unique style or method of working. They were very resistant to following directions and trying new techniques, mediums, materials, and methods. Interestingly, art is one of the only college majors where some students come in with a chip on their shoulder. Why is this, you might ask? Because unlike language arts, math, and science, art is often NOT taught in Elementary, middle school, and high school. Instead, pre-college art students were allowed to have free time to draw, paint, and sculpt whatever they wanted and earned a participation grade instead of receiving real instruction and critiques.

Conversely, language arts, math, and science majors have had twelve years of their papers, tests, and essays marked up with a red pen and told to revise, re-write, recalculate, re-think, and redo. Art students have NOT had their work corrected or honestly critiqued by competent teachers preparing them for a career in art.

Many college freshmen and sophomore art students are surprised when their art instructors begin teaching design principles. Many of these students struggle when they are required to illustrate a narrative or concept. Instead of being able to start a piece of art with no end or purpose, many become

paralyzed or angry with the limitations and requirements placed on their work. I've seen many illustrators change majors during this transition simply because they were never prepared for the hard work of illustration.

My advice is to surrender to the process. Let go. Don't try to drive the ship. Allow your teachers to teach. The best artists are usually the best students. The best students have learned to be humble and teachable. To use an obvious metaphor, they are like the sponge. You are going to have teachers you do not like, teachers who aren't as capable or competent as they could or should be. Try to find the kernels of wisdom or knowledge that they possess. You might not learn much from some of them, but through practice, time, note-taking and conversation, you can maintain your humility and your thirst for learning from the teachers who will teach you a lot.

There just aren't that many shortcuts to learning—you just need to fall in love with the process.

> Making art is hard. It's easy to have fun making marks in your sketchbook or tablet. Sitting down and working through the concept, design challenges, and execution of an image isn't easy. When the going gets tough, many art students procrastinate by finding something more fun to do.

Fall in love with art making

Doodling, sketching, and messing around with paint is easy. Making art is *hard*. It's easy to have fun making marks in your sketchbook or tablet. Sitting down and working through the concept, design challenges, and execution of an image isn't easy. When the going gets tough, many art students procrastinate by finding something more fun to do.

Successful art students have figured out that making a great piece of art is more fun than a video game. There's no feeling like looking at a piece of art you created, starting from a blank canvas or sheet of paper. Knowing that you have worked the problem and succeeded and having the evidence to show is priceless. I don't know any artists who were born having fun *making* art—instead, the master artists I know taught themselves over time to enjoy every aspect of the creative process.

Each year I taught at University, I noticed that some of my students were ten to fifteen minutes late starting their in-class drawing or painting assignments almost every day. They dawdled and chatted up other students as they slowly got their materials ready, while other students came in, got ready, and began the assignment quickly. These same slow students were the same students who packed up fifteen minutes early each day. I concluded that they liked being an illustration major, but didn't like illustrating. Show me someone who doesn't like illustrating and I'll show you someone who won't become an illustrator.

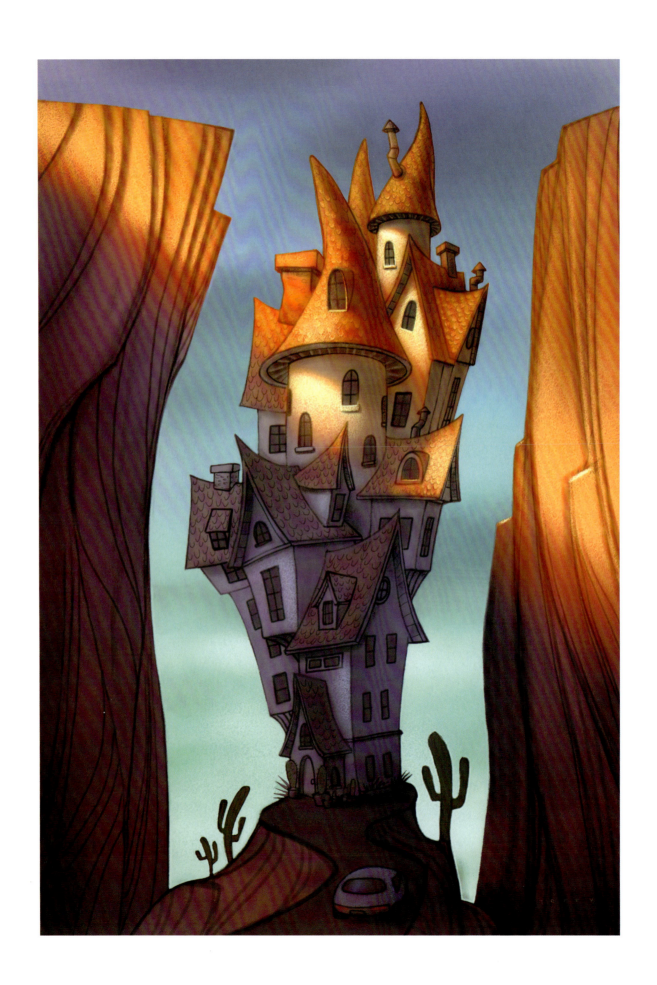

> **The more you care about your work, the more you will love your work and the easier it will be to spend time on the less "fun" but necessary parts of your work.**

When I was a student, I used to hate the design phase. I skipped crucial planning that needed to be done in the drawing phase to get to the painting. Over time and through a lot of frustration at my failed paintings, I realized the importance of careful image planning and design. Designing my images has become equally enjoyable because I can visualize what my painting is going to look like before I start painting. The more you care about your work, the more you will *love* your work and the easier it will be to spend time on the less "fun" but necessary parts of your work.

Become friends with your teachers

Many of your art teachers have past or current freelance and/or in-house work experience in the markets you want to work in. They have experience doing many of the things you will be challenged with when you finish school. Some of your teachers will be forthcoming with their knowledge while others will not. If you work hard in class, listen, and take their critique advice, you will impress them. It will be easy for you to ask them questions pertaining to your art career because you will know that they appreciate your hard work. It will be easier for them to invest time in you because they know they aren't wasting their time.

I am friends with many of my teachers from college and we often go out to grab a bite to eat. I have had access to them in past decades because I have worked to cultivate our relationship. After I finished my BFA, I made appointments to meet with a few of them because I had many questions about pursuing a career in freelance illustration. Without their help, I don't think I'd be an illustrator today.

In addition, I'm friends with many of my former students. Some have become teachers and have come to me to get advice on teaching; but most have asked and continue to ask me for advice on their careers or projects that they are working on. Many of my students have taught *me* valuable lessons as well—for example, in selling my work with new technology and creating my work using new digital tools. Some of my very best friends are my former students!

Network with your peers

Some of the students in your class are going to be really good at art. Some of them are going to be really helpful in explaining the concepts from your classes. Some of them are like you—they want to be friends with the most committed artists in class. Some of them will want to partner with other artists in the future to produce a product. Some of them might end up working for a company that is looking to hire another artist like you. Some of them will work in the same freelance markets you'd like to work for and can offer advice. Some of them will become teachers who will need to recommend other artists when new teaching positions become available.

I've noticed that many students like to come into class and play the mysterious "artist in hoodie with headphones" role. I've always tried to help them see that they are missing out on the wealth of opportunity that getting to know their fellow students offers. Also, I've never seen the hoodie artist ever make it as a freelance illustrator. You could almost say that those who shut themselves out from their peers will just not make it as a professional artist.

Your classmates can tell you what you missed when you were absent. They can tell you what you missed when you weren't paying attention. You can debate the details of the assignment rules with them. They can give you feedback before the big critique. They can invite you to go with them to art lectures and shows and they can help you remember upcoming deadlines. It's foolish to ignore what I call "half of your education"—that is, networking with your peers. You're paying for it after all.

Learn to take a critique

Spending time on your art, only to have someone tell you what you did wrong, is frustrating for every beginning artist. In addition, it's often 180 degrees from the praise most beginners are used to getting after completing a painting. However, without honest feedback you cannot learn to improve. I have found that many students aren't able to actually hear a critique of their work because they haven't yet learned that their work is disposable.

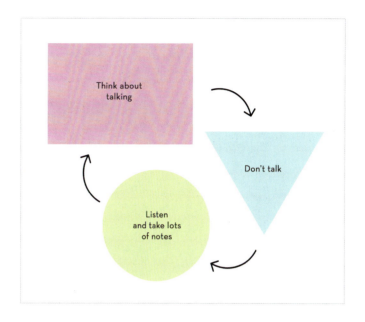

Young artists often place a very high value on each piece they create, even if it's just a sketch. They haven't learned that they are a fountain and, if successful, will create thousands of pieces of work in their lifetime. They need to learn that not everything they touch is precious. Visual artists need to learn to be more like musicians, actors, and athletes. Musicians practice a part of a song and then it evaporates and they get feedback from their instructor or band members. Theater performers are the same—they say their lines many times in practice. Basketball players run drills over and over; however, if they only focus on that beautiful 3-pointer they made last month but their overall shooting percentage is low, it's a loser mentality.

What is the equivalent "practice" for an animator or illustrator? It's making drawing after drawing and forgetting about them afterwards. Just because you left a "receipt" (doodle, drawing, or sketch) doesn't mean it has value. As soon as you can view your work as (disposable) exercises and a means to getting better, you will have the mindset to receive a critique.

You know an artist is having a hard time accepting a critique when that artist constantly interrupts the teacher/peer on every point and/or explains why the teacher/peer is wrong. What the argumentative student doesn't realize is that he or she is unwittingly teaching the teacher and/or peers that it's a waste of time to offer honest feedback. It's a waste of time to care or put any thought into helping the know-it-all student. The immature student is killing his chances of learning in the class because nobody likes a know-it-all. Nobody is going to be willing to invest in you if you can't even invest in *yourself* by simply listening.

An honest critique is a gift. It is time and attention from someone who is taking a risk in possibly offending you in order to help you achieve your goals. Even if you disagree with a critique, try to have the humility to take notes and thank the person giving the critique. There is no cost to keep your thoughts to yourself. You do not have to take the advice; and yes, some of it will be bad, but you will scare away the good advice if you do not learn to invite a critique.

If you really want to get someone's HONEST feedback, try saying something like, "I really want your honest feedback. I cannot get better if you just tell me what you like about my drawing/painting. Please feel free to tell me the top three things you'd change, so I can take notes." That's a winning attitude and the person you're talking to will feel much safer telling you the truth…which is what you want.

> An honest critique is a gift. It is time and attention from someone who is taking a risk in possibly offending you in order to help you achieve your goals.

Learn to give a critique

Anyone can criticize an artist's painting but it takes an artful approach to give a meaningful and constructive critique. Many feel that you should find something nice to say about a person's work before you tell them what you think is NOT working. It usually makes the suggested changes go down easier when a few compliments are offered first. But what if you can't think of anything good to say about the work in front of you? You can say something like, "I think I know what you're trying to say here," or "I like the direction you're taking on this." It's a good persuasion strategy to make the artist feel comfortable with you first and assure them that your intent is not to hurt them.

If you're going to give a critique to someone who is new to criticism, you should limit your comments to three to five points. Many times, you can find ten to twenty or more things wrong with student work, but you will only frustrate and confuse (and possibly break) an artist with too many criticisms. Rome wasn't built in a day and neither is an artist or his portfolio. Just give the artist a few things to work on, and address other problems in future projects.

In order to *get* good critiques, it's important to learn to *give* them. I've had students who come late to class missing most of the critiques, but at the same time want their work talked about. How is this fair? Most art teachers expect their students to participate in the critique of their fellow students' work. If you are late or if you choose to remain silent during critiques and expect your work to be critiqued, you are being selfish. You need to be willing to "make a deposit" and risk offending your peers in order to "make the withdrawal" of receiving a critique—it's only fair.

You might not make the most intelligent comments and your teacher might disagree with your suggestions, but you will learn so much more by participating.

Online school vs art school

If we're going to talk about how to be the best art student, we should probably discuss the options that art students have. Unless you've been asleep for the past ten years, you probably know that there are many more options for learning art than there were just a decade ago.

In addition to the brick and mortar schools around the world, there are now many online options. Some online art schools offer full degree programs while others only offer instruction. The question is, "What's right for you?"

Unlike other college majors where the piece of paper is just as important as the school you went to, it's ultimately about your portfolio in art. It's rare that an artist lands a job because they went to a prestigious art school. Employers in publishing, animation, comics, advertising, and design want to see what you can do. You will never be turned down for a freelance assignment based on your lack of education; in fact, *where* you went to school and *if* you have a degree never enters the conversation. If an art buyer at a company sees your work and thinks you would be perfect for the job, the discussion revolves around your availability and negotiations about your payment.

Many of the top freelancers today are either "self-taught" or they pieced their art education together through online options. I would imagine, though, that most successful studio and freelance artists attended a brick and mortar art school; however, each year more and more artists are turning to online offerings.

One of the biggest benefits to attending a physical school is the face-to face-attention and feedback you will receive from your teachers. One of the biggest drawbacks, however, is that you cannot choose some of your teachers. Often there is only one teacher teaching the class you need. You are relying on the school to hire the best teachers they can find. Sometimes a school can't find the best, so they settle on a less-qualified or less engaging teacher. This is where online has an advantage.

With online art school options, you can pick and choose the classes from the teachers you want sourced from the entire *world*. You have access to teachers you would never be able to afford to travel to. You can choose when to watch their class, where to watch their class, how long to watch their class, and when to complete your work. All of this freedom comes at a tiny fraction of the cost as well.

Some students are self-motivated and will work hard on their own time without procrastinating—these students would probably do well learning online in a self-directed approach. Other students are not self-motivated yet, and need the threat of a bad grade to motivate them to work on their assignments. You have to decide what's right for you. Many students do both by supplementing their degree program with online classes to fill in gaps.

> **Unlike other college majors where the piece of paper is just as important as the school you went to, it's ultimately about your portfolio in art. It's rare that an artist lands a job because they went to a prestigious art school.**

I don't know what market I want to work in?

This is a common question and I struggled with it when I was in school in 1988. Would I be a graphic designer, a cartoonist, an illustrator of children's books, an animator, or an editorial artist? Or would I illustrate cereal boxes or make art for bed spreads, wrapping paper, and decorative bags? Greeting cards, maybe? "How am I supposed to know exactly what I want to do right now," you may be asking yourself. The good news is that you do NOT have to pick one…well, not for life, anyway. If you are going into an art school program, you WILL have to decide between animation and illustration, or graphic design, fine art, sculpture, printmaking, etc. The good news is that all of them teach very similar principles.

It would be fairly easy to transition back and forth from graphic design to illustration or over to animation even though you didn't go through a 4-year program in each one. The idea that you picked the "wrong one" and are forever stuck in a market or field that you don't want is false. Again, online options are the solution to many 4-year degree grads that want to make a lane change after school.

When I started freelancing in the early 90s, illustrators often only worked in one market. I knew a lot of editorial illustrators, advertising illustrators, children's book illustrators, and greeting card illustrators. Rarely did any of my friends work cross-market. In other words, they just did editorial work or advertising work, etc.

All of that has now changed for many reasons, but more of my illustrator friends take assignments from many different markets. Take Jake Parker, for instance. He has worked in animation, illustrated Rocket Raccoon for Marvel, along with many children's books. Jake also illustrates his own graphic novels and has made character designs for many companies. He also created Inktober and co-founded SVSLearn.com with me!

If you don't know what market you want to pursue, just pick a project you've always wanted to do such as a children's book, a comic, board game, or puzzle. Pick a project you can fall in love with and work your guts out on making it the best _____ you can make. Your project will teach you more lessons than you can imagine, and it will get you moving.

> **Pick a project you can fall in love with and work your guts out on making it the best _____ you can make. Your project will teach you more lessons than you can imagine, and it will get you moving.**

You will learn what you like and don't like about working in that area and you will have to solve problems you didn't know how to solve at first. You might learn that you never want to make a _____ again or you might find that you want to make a sequel! Projects get attention, especially if you share them on social media (assuming it's a really well-done project) and you never know what other work they could lead to.

HOW TO BE SUCCESSFUL IN ART SCHOOL

"Most art consumers want more than a pretty picture—they want you to *say* something. They want you to speak to their souls."

BECOMING A MASTER ARTIST

What is art?

Most young artists confuse craft with art—meaning that they value the ability to draw or paint but they undervalue the *purpose* for drawing or painting. A good example would be drawing a child sitting in a chair. The drawing could be academically and anatomically correct and the technique flawless and masterful. However, some would value it more if the child sitting in the chair was facing a corner looking back with a tear running down his or her cheek. This is because the second drawing shows a familiar story and familiar stories speak to our hearts as we have shared similar experiences. This is not to say that you cannot move someone emotionally with craft but it is often much more difficult.

I prefer to define art as something that can change one emotionally. If you cannot alter your viewers' emotions, they won't care about your art. Think of the novels, movies, plays, comedy routines, and music that you love vs. the ones you hated, or simply cannot remember. The art that you love made you laugh, cry, get angry, fear, feel empathy, and/or many other emotions.

The movies you cannot remember probably didn't do much to stimulate your mind emotionally.

Many artists who struggle to earn a living with their art have not learned this very important lesson. I have known many artists who are phenomenal with a paint brush or pencil—they can render perfect human figures, trees, leaves, and tiny details—yet they fail to create interesting concepts or stories with their illustrations. These artists usually define art as that which is rendered and crafted as perfectly as possible. Unfortunately, most art consumers want more than a pretty picture—they want you to *say* something. They want you to speak to their souls.

I have sold a lot of fan art at comic conventions since 2016. I chose to create an original backstory to the pop culture characters I drew. Instead of just drawing the characters in my style, I answered the question, "What would they have done when they were little?" By doing so, I created a very popular line of characters. At most conventions, I was more successful than the artists around me because my art made people laugh when they viewed the unexpected concept. It was a joy to listen to customers pointing, laughing, and telling their friends, "Ooh—look at Wolverine...he's chopping broccoli," or "Captain America is riding on his flying saucer shield!"

> **To create art, you need to master the craft and THEN you need to tell a unique story or concept to move people emotionally.**

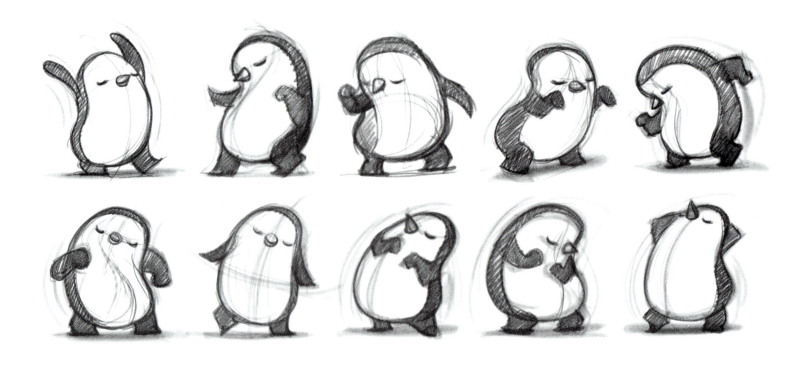

To create art, you need to master the craft and THEN you need to tell a unique story or concept to move people emotionally.

Your capacity for working longer on an image will increase

In the early stages of the artistic journey, most artists aren't able to work on a drawing or painting longer than fifteen minutes to an hour. Perhaps they will work on their art longer than that in a single day, but usually they will bounce to a new drawing or painting as they feel they have done all they can on the previous image. Many art students will "finish" their class assignments before the allotted time is up, saying they can't see anything else that needs to be worked on.

In school, students learn that master painters and illustrators can work for forty to one-hundred hours or more on a single painting. Some students might be afraid they will never increase their ability to work this long on a single image. *(Note: Keep in mind that a master artist has evolved to a high degree of efficiency, so fifty hours from a master is probably equivalent to more than one-hundred hours for an amateur.)*

Rest assured that the more you dedicate yourself to improving the fundamentals of design, drawing, and rendering, the better you will be able to naturally identify work that needs to be corrected and re-corrected in your work. One hour will easily become two; two will become four, and so on.

You will be amazed at the transformation your

> You will be able to spend more time on your work because as you improve, you will be so excited to continue working on a painting or drawing that's turning out better than you imagined. It's one of the "highs" that artists constantly seek.

mind will achieve as you strive for excellence in your work. In a few years, you'll look back at your one-hour images and easily see how much more work you could have put into them if you had had the brain you have today.

The longest painting I ever worked on took me close to one-hundred hours and they were some of the easiest, most rewarding hours I have ever spent on one painting at that time in my illustration career. You will be able to spend more time on your work because as you improve, you will be so excited to continue working on a painting or drawing that's turning out better than you imagined. It's one of the "highs" that artists constantly seek.

Never get comfortable with your art

One thing many master artists have in common is that almost all of them went through a period where they thought they had "arrived" or "made it" only to be followed up by the realization that they still had so much to learn. If you find an artist who is stuck in the mindset that their art is "the best it's going to be" or "this is how I do it" mode, you'll find an artist who has ceased to progress. There's only one direction when an artist gets stuck in this phase—backwards. In fact, all of the artists I know who got stuck there aren't working as artists anymore.

If you aren't innovating and taking risks (and changing people emotionally), you aren't creating art; and if you aren't creating art, you're bound to eventually lose interest since your audience will slowly but surely lose interest.

How do you avoid getting comfortable? First, I think you need to get comfortable with the fact that to become a great artist, you need to constantly learn new techniques, principles, methods, etc. As an artist, you are on a never-ending quest to create the unattainable perfect work of art. It's out there, but you will never fully reach it—and that's fine.

Second, I think you should put away your past artwork and set a personal goal to outperform it every year. The best artists are a fountain of creativity because they challenge their past perceptions with new information, new experiences, new opinions, and new associations. If you aren't replacing your old work every year or two, you are stagnating.

I've given portfolio reviews at conferences many times and sometimes I've revisited the same conferences years later. I know when an artist has become a hobbyist because their portfolio does not change even after many years have gone by. **If you want to be a pro, you have to ditch that old work every year or every few years and replace it with your new, better work.**

Copying is one of the best ways to improve

Copying is almost never looked at in a positive light. Nobody likes it when a comedian rips off someone else's joke or you catch someone on social media passing off someone else's art as their own. Copying another artist's hard work is usually synonymous with theft.

However, what most artists don't know or only learn later in their pursuit of excellence is that making a copy of a master artist's work is not only important, it's essential to your development as an artist. The difference is that when you make a master's copy for learning purposes, you just need to make sure that anyone who sees it knows you're not claiming it as an original work.

But why is it so important to make a master's copy? Let's examine other art mediums to see how this concept can relate to visual art. In basketball and football, athletes often run pre-designed plays that were designed by master players. Sure, players must learn to be creative and make their own

How do you avoid getting comfortable?

First, get comfortable with the fact that to become a great artist, you need to constantly learn new techniques, principles, methods, etc.

As an artist, you are on a never-ending quest to create the unattainable perfect work of art. It's out there, but you will never fully reach it—and that's fine.

Second, put away your past artwork and set a personal goal to outperform it every year.

moves, but often a designed play is used. Musicians in an orchestra play music written by a master composer. Sculptors often work at foundries, apprenticing for years, helping the master artists cast their sculptures in bronze. In each case, the final product is not the sole creation of one artist; there's a collaboration even though, more often than not, the master is the one who gets most or all of the credit.

In order to learn, you must see art through the eyes and hands of those who came before you. By copying, you can get into the mind of the master artist. Copying will allow you to get answers to the creation of a work you admire. You will never be the same artist after dedicating yourself to the many hours it takes to make a master's copy...you are forever changed.

When making a master's copy, your goal should be to confuse your viewers to the point that they cannot tell original from fake. This means you must be committed to go the distance, to recreate every detail! It will take you longer to make a copy than it took for the master because you will not be efficient at his or her process. It might take you longer than you have ever worked on something before—that's

a good thing. However, if you put the time into making the copied art as perfect as possible, you will learn some very powerful lessons.

Structure your life to inspire your art

Artists often do not recognize the relationship between their lived experiences and the creation of their art. If you think about it, however, it's not hard to realize that in order to make great art, you have to have a wide variety of experiences. Think of the visual art you like to consume…what is the subject matter? Landscapes? Figurative work? Narrative illustration? Is there conflict in the work that you like? Drama? I'm a children's book illustrator and I need to relate to the characters I'm drawing and their situations in order for me to successfully tell their stories.

No matter what, your life experiences will manifest in your work—good or bad. The artist who spends his or her time indoors will have a harder time creating the feeling and the mood of the outdoors and vice versa. The more experiences you have through your life, the more versatile your work can be. Jake Parker, a well-known illustrator, refers to your experiences and the art you consume as your "creative bank account." Like any account, you cannot make withdrawals without first making deposits.

My advice is to try to keep an open mindset. Try to be open to new experiences, new friends, new activities, new environments, and new trips. Hike a new trail, drive different routes to get home, talk to people you might not normally talk to, volunteer for work you don't normally do. You'll be amazed at how new experiences will find their way into your work, even if only subtly.

I sometimes hear students say, "I'm stuck—I don't know what to draw." "I don't know what I want to do for a personal project." "What do you think I should do?"

My answer is always the same, "You need to start living…get out there!"

You must sacrifice for your art

Every world class athlete, doctor, lawyer, and, yes—artist, has chosen to give up things they enjoy to become great at what they do. For me, I realized that if I was going to be able to compete with my classmates, I was going to have to spend more time on my art. This meant that I was going to have to take time away from things I was used to doing. I gave up some of my tv shows, video games, watching sports, and some of my racquetball time.

Art directors are tasked with finding the best talent on budget who can meet their deadlines. Galleries are looking for the best art that they think their clientele will purchase. Studios have an abundance of artists applying for work each year, and they are able to pick from the top of the top.

Two things are true:

> 1. *I believe just about anyone can become a professional artist earning a living with their craft if they dedicate their life to it.*
>
> 2. *In order to become a pro, you have to be willing to work harder than most other artists; and in order to work harder, you have to be willing to give up or sacrifice some of the things that you love.*

How much sacrifice is required? As much as it takes for you to develop your craft and style to the point where businesses such as galleries, publishers, ad agencies, and studios think that they can make money with your art.

Most of us have some degree of dishonest self-talk. You know how it goes—you say to yourself something like, "I'll just have a few more cookies because I had a hard day and I deserve them." Honest self-talk would be more like, "It's been a long day and I'm weak. I know I shouldn't have more cookies, but right now I don't care that I'm putting my health at risk. I value the taste and feeling of eating cookies more."

The reason I bring up dishonest self-talk is that I often hear students tell me what they are *not* willing to give up instead of the other way around—for example: "It's Friday night and I always do something fun with my friends. I shouldn't be expected to sacrifice my Friday nights." When we hold on to these "sacred cows", we lie to ourselves and thereby cheat ourselves of the sacrifices necessary to become great.

I'm not saying you can't have a Friday night off, but if you have a list of five-to-ten "I can't be expected to give up" things, you probably have a dishonest self-talk and you probably aren't truly dedicated to becoming a professional artist.

My art never turns out how I envisioned it

You are not alone! Almost every artist experiences this in his or her early creative years. You get an idea so you start to sketch it out, but you can't quite get the drawing right, so you start to render it out with color…but when you are finished, it doesn't come close to the original vision you had in your mind. If you get frustrated every time this happens, that's a great thing! It means that you *care,* and caring about your work is necessary to improve your art. How many people have tried drawing and/or painting who just didn't care how it turned out? Billions? And guess what they aren't doing for a living right now?

Let's take *you*, on the other hand. You're ambitious and you have dreams of creating amazing works of art that will make the world more enjoyable. How do you get past this phase? How do you start recreating your art visions in a visual form for others to see?

Ira Glass wrote about this. He explained that when you start out, you have good taste. You have a natural aesthetic that is intrinsic to you, but you haven't developed the ability to express that taste in an art form. But, he explains, if you stick with it long enough, and make enough mistakes—and continually try to learn from them and improve—you will one day develop the skills to render your ideas as you envisioned them.

> **If you stick with it long enough, and make enough mistakes—and continually try to learn from them and improve—you will one day develop the skills to render your ideas as you envisioned them.**

I like to think of it this way: You have hundreds, if not thousands of bad paintings in you—every artist does. So, you need to get busy making them so you can put them aside and get on with making the art you dreamed of. Writers are often given the advice to write their novel and then throw it away and start from scratch. The idea is that the first round will be a mess, but you will know your story so much better and will be able to tell it more efficiently without the distractions and superfluous elements.

Should I work digitally or traditionally?

Gallery artists probably don't consider this question in their quest for mediums, but let's explore the pros and cons of working each way, for illustrators.

Working traditionally in a natural medium like watercolor or acrylic paint is still a valid way to work. Many illustrators use traditional mediums to work in publishing, advertising, editorial, and design; however, they are becoming a small minority as digital has become the most popular method. Traditional mediums also seem to enable beginning artists to establish more unique textures than digital tools. The biggest advantage of working traditionally is that you have an original that you can display or sell. Because traditional mediums have become much rarer, art directors, editors, and creative directors have been known to excitedly pour into the conference room to "ooh and ahh" over original, traditionally-rendered work that has just arrived at their office.

Working digitally is actually the preferred method most companies want their illustrators to use. Simply put, they want it fast, editable, and they don't want to take responsibility for damage, loss, or theft. Companies that buy art on a regular basis have had to pay lots of times when something went wrong, and some of them will only work with digital artists (or artists who can deliver digital files). You can work traditionally if you can make digital copies—or are willing to pay for them—that you can upload to these clients.

Working digitally is generally faster for most professional artists who used to work traditionally; therefore, you can take on more work and make more money. It's often easier to work remotely when you go digital. I use a Wacom Cintiq monitor to draw and paint on in the office, but I can complete all of my design and drawing work anywhere in the world on my iPad. I've gotten a lot of work done in doctor's offices, on planes, and in hotel rooms.

Probably the biggest advantage you get with digital is the edit-ability of your work. With layers and "undo," you can pretty much rule the world! Ahh, but it comes at a cost. Beginning artists need to develop a process that they can repeat. Like a baking recipe, if you don't follow the process exactly, the end result could flop.

When learning to design, draw, and paint digitally, most students have great difficulty repeating their process because they rely too heavily on *layers* and "undo." Each digital painting has a different process with a different number of layers and a different set of tools used. I've seen students with fifty layers or more! If you look at the digital files from the top pro illustrators, you will notice very few layers in comparison and sometimes just a few layers.

I suggest that students begin with traditional mediums to learn in a more natural way. When you were a toddler learning to walk you made good and bad moves. Bad moves usually ended in a fall while good moves moved you towards the toy on the other side of the room. When you fell, it hurt and your brain tried to figure out what you did wrong—mistake and correction. When you excessively use layers and undo, you cheat the pain process and you do not feel the consequences. The consequence or pain is what drives you to make necessary changes that will later become natural to your method.

Many of the best digital artists have transferred their traditional methods to digital tools which has enabled them to recreate their process digitally. Their style often looks more unique because their approach to using digital tools came from a traditional process.

If you want to go directly to digital, you might find success by limiting the tools you can use. Try one brush paintings with no eraser, no undo and work on one layer. This will force you to think like someone painting with oils on a canvas.

Is my artwork good enough?

No. I mean, it's never good enough—right? Good enough for what? To stop learning? No, it's never good enough to think you have arrived. That's the death of an artist. I know, you probably mean "is it good enough to get paid work?" Maybe. There are multiple factors at work to determine this question.

First, does it fit in with your favorite professional artists? Does it stand up to their work? To determine this, first you need eight pro artists that you really admire. If you can't rattle off eight, you need to start consuming more great art. In order to be great, you have to know what great is. Do you think that there isn't a college-bound basketball athlete who can't list eight of their favorite pro basketball players? Start with Instagram because almost every world class illustrator can be found there.

> **It could be that you are good—but not quite good enough to turn the heads of art buyers and gallery owners who see great art every single day.** *Your work has to interrupt their day in a great way.*

Second, create a nine-box grid of squares with your art in the center, and art from your eight favorite pros in the squares around it. This should help you see how your work compares in concept, design, craft, and style. Sometimes it's hard to identify exactly where your work falls short. Try to take an accurate inventory by making a list—the more specific the better. You might want to ask a trusted artist to look at your nine-box grid and tell you what you need to change to bring your work up to the level of the other eight.

Third, keep in mind that attracting work from paying clients is much harder than keeping a paying client you've already landed. What I mean is that those illustrators who are already working—the ones who are inking or drawing comics, illustrating children's books and graphic novels, or already represented by galleries—have it much easier than you. They are already taking up space and if they are easy to work with, on time, and really good, there isn't much incentive for a client to pick you instead of them.

Often I'm shown really great work by an artist who then explains that they just aren't getting much or any work yet. It could be that they aren't visible enough. It could be that they are good—but not quite good enough to turn the heads of art buyers and gallery owners who see great art every single day. You see the sky every day to the point that you expect it. Gallery owners are desensitized to great artwork because they see it every day. This doesn't mean that they aren't always looking for new and fresh flavor, but your work has to interrupt their day in a great way. New talent is discovered every day.

In the meantime, I suggest that artists get busy working on their own art projects, and posting their progress online. It's much easier to attract an audience when you have an ongoing project to talk about rather than an unrelated drawing here and a painting there. Projects lead to client work, and I'll talk about that more in the chapter, *"Creating Your Own Brand."*

How can I get feedback on my work?

I often get this question from artists who have finished school, are taking online view-only classes, or are just working on their portfolios in their own time. Getting feedback is *essential* to improving your artwork and you'll probably never be able to go pro without it. Here are a few ideas:

1. ***Participate in online forums.*** *There are several vibrant communities of artists online where sharing art and getting feedback is standard. At SVSLearn.com, there is a forum where children's book illustrators are constantly helping each other.*

2. ***Form a critique group.*** *Critique groups are a common way writers and illustrators cooperate to give valuable opinions on each other's work. It isn't easy finding the right members for your group; however, it's gotten a lot easier since the Internet's invention. You can form a group that meets in person or online. Often, meeting online is the only option, but through digital tools like Google or Skype, it's very possible to meet with artists all over the world.*

3. ***Buy a critique from a pro.*** *There are individual mentors and professional artists willing to sell their time online to help you achieve your goals. They might not all be easy to find on a Google search, but* ***get into an illustration forum and you'll get plenty of suggestions.***

4. ***Attend an SCBWI Conference.*** *You'll have to check the website of your local SCBWI (Society of Children's Book Writers and Illustrators) regions, because some of their events cater to writers only. Once or twice a year, however, they will gear a conference towards illustrators.*

BECOMING A MASTER ARTIST

Sometimes they have art directors visit from publishing hubs like NYC to critique portfolios. Those are priceless opportunities, even with a potential $50 price tag, because you'll get a critique from a real-life editor, art director, illustrator, or creative director in the business. There are also two HUGE national conferences for SCBWI each year—one on the U.S. east coast and one on the west coast.

5. ***Buy an online class that includes critiques.***
Some online classes come with built-in critiques for the homework assigned. These classes come at a higher price but often they are much, much cheaper than an a-la-carte university or art school program. Besides, most of the time you can't choose to enroll in an upper level class at an art school without being fully accepted into their program.

Teaching—to improve your work

One of the best ways to learn a process is to explain that process to someone else. If you know that you are going to have to explain something, you either study and practice up so you can go through the steps, or you fail. How do you teach the steps if you don't know them? Well first, you obviously have to gain the knowledge, and that can take time but it really depends on what level you're trying to teach. A high school art student who is serious about their art can teach an elementary school child—they may not be able to teach a child everything, but enough to help them improve. A college art student can teach a high school student and a college art school grad (who is very serious) can teach a college art student.

The higher you go in art, the more discoveries and epiphanies you will have that are unique to your methods and your style. You'll develop theories and ideas that you weren't taught. It gets really fun when you try to break your personal discoveries down to try to explain them. When you do, your understanding of your own discoveries will compound into more discoveries. Trying to describe what comes naturally to you is where the deep learning is for both you and your student or mentee.

When you figure out how to break it down, you force yourself to rehearse and memorize. You lock it in.

Many artists don't think they're qualified to teach so they don't try, but they are missing out on one of life's inherent truths—teaching makes you better. You might not be qualified to teach a high school or college art class, but you can probably help elementary or junior high students. There is a caveat, however; you have to care about your student more than yourself. In other words, you have to *teach* well enough for them to learn something; if your focus is on them, you both benefit.

Don't be a generalist

In general, I'm going to give you advice on NOT being a generalist because most of the highly successful artists are specialists. A generalist is someone who is good at a lot of things, but not *great* at any one thing. A hundred years ago, when there were family farms dotting the countryside, farmers had to be good at preparing the land for crops, planting, weeding, irrigating, pest control, and fixing all their machinery. They had to know how to do a little of everything to run the farm. Today, there are seed experts and even experts for each type of seed. There are weed control experts and irrigation systems

experts and there are farm machinery mechanics and probably thousands of experts that service the farming community.

In order to stand out, you need to work to perfect your signature style. When you have a style that feels fresh and unique and has a professional polish to it, you will begin to attract your audience. Over time you can become known as the person who does _____, and that's exactly what you want! You want people to refer to you as "you know, the gal who paints dogs as famous baseball players" or "that guy who has a really dark drawing with really light pastel colors radiating from behind." People will refer to you that way when you have developed a large body of similar work and it's getting seen.

Developing your own style

How do you develop a unique style that art buyers will find appealing? Most experts agree that every artist has a unique style because each one of us has a unique taste. Here's how to start: First, identify three to five professional artists whose work you like the most. Second, make a list of the specific attributes for each artist that make their work appealing to you. For instance, if you like Jon Klassen's style, you might note things like defined shapes, white backgrounds, limited muted colors, strong silhouettes, and texture.

Once you have your list from three to five artists, you can begin to make an amalgam of their work. Take a few things from each artist and create your own unique amalgam of stylistic elements. Viewers should be able to see who is influencing your work, but not feel that it's a direct rip off of one artist's work. Throughout history, artists have apprenticed and studied under master artists. You can easily look at the greatest painters and sculptors in the history books and see who they were influenced by.

Now comes the hard part. You have to *work* for years for a few things to happen. First, you will start to form your own methods of creation. They might be subtle, but after mechanically implementing your list of style attributes, you will naturally begin to evolve into your way of thinking. This will happen over the years so you won't notice it happening, but others will probably point it out for you.

BECOMING A MASTER ARTIST

The last things that will happen is that you will forget about your list. You will begin working on a piece and it will be *yours* from start to finish. You'll probably also notice imitators of your work if you are successful. It can be flattering and a bit threatening at the same time.

If you are in school or just finished and are a few years into your career as a pro, keep in mind that it often takes five to ten years for an artist to really find their style. The process I described will help speed it up a little; but, if you are serious and committed, you will get there—because each of us is unique and has a unique style waiting to get out. Are you willing to go far enough to release it?

"You will 'make it' if you are constantly making it—art, that is. In other words, you need to concentrate on a consistent life of making art and, more importantly, always making *better* art."

GETTING FREELANCE WORK AFTER ART SCHOOL

Will I make it?

This is the burning question all of us have had or currently have, right? Will I be able to have a successful career with my art? I know what it's like to not know if you're going to make it as an illustrator because I worried that my efforts would not pay off. Allow me to offer another way to think about "making it" or being a successful artist.

Many of the most celebrated artists from world history were unable to earn a living with their art and many only achieved notoriety after death. Some of our most famous illustrators and animators were barely able to put food on the table with their art. For various reasons, many artists have been unable or unwilling—or simply lacked the knowledge—to command higher wages or commissions for their work.

We as artists are often passionate and enthusiastic about our work and that has made us an easy target for savvy businessmen and women. Our desire to do the thing we love is often easily exploited because we would work for free at times just to see our work printed with a credit!

A better way to think about "making it" is to measure your efforts by the time you put into your craft and the improvements you make each year. If you determine your worth based on external influences such as a paid assignment, you might also allow yourself to believe that your work is more valuable than it actually is. If you get lucky and get paid three to five times your normal commission price, did the art suddenly become more valuable?

You will "make it" if you are constantly making it—art, that is. In other words, you need to concentrate on a consistent life of making art and, more importantly, always making *better* art. That is how you will feel fulfilled as an artist—when you are able to execute the vision you had of the art you just made. Ironically, the artists who make the best art (satisfying their own desires) and who promote that art are usually the artists who earn the most money...but what is "the best art?"

What is freelance work?

"Freelance work" refers to work assignments you get from a company or individual in which you are typically only hired for one project or period of time. In most cases, when the project ends, your assignment and payment(s) also end. Instead of being hired "in house" with benefits, a freelancer usually works from their home or office and must pay for all of their own utilities and supplies.

The artist has a client/contractor relationship. The company is the artist's client and the contractor is the company's associate. Most illustration work is assigned to freelance illustrators as opposed to in-house artists.

What kind of freelance work is out there? Let's look at the various markets where freelance illustrators are finding work:

Publishing:	*Children's books, picture books, big books, chapter books, board books, comics, graphic novels, text books, and activity books*
Products:	*Board games, video games, puzzles, card games, greeting cards, etc.*
Advertising:	*Video spots, ads in magazines and across media, brochures, flyers, mailers*
Design/packaging:	*Bottle and jar labels, boxes, bags, totes, sleeves, containers*
Editorial:	*Stories in magazines and newspapers, including digital formats*
Institutional:	*Murals, annual reports, theatre posters, music posters, corporate literature, foundation documents*
Licensing:	*Illustrations used to decorate products such as gift bags, gift wrap, shower curtains, pillow cases, bed spreads, curtains, table cloths, flags, fabric, etc.*

How do you get freelance work?

Getting freelance illustration work is hard in the beginning, but if you are creating your best work, it gets easier with time. Basically, there are only two factors: Is your work great, and, do the people who make art assignments know you exist? The first factor means constantly working on your portfolio to get it competition-ready. The second takes a bit of knowledge, so let's dive in.

You can look for work on your own or you can hire what's called a "rep" in the business or an agent if you are writing and/or illustrating. Some artists do both, but many reps don't want their "talent" looking for work as they don't want to compete for assignments with their artists. A rep manages advertising/marketing, portfolio updates including the illustrator's website, contracts, and billing, and sends the illustrator the appropriate percentage when the assignment is completed. I'll discuss how to find a rep in a later chapter.

To get freelance work in general, you need to get your work in front of both editors and art directors (and hopefully the creative director as well). This can be accomplished in a variety of ways.

Looking for work on your own

Finding work is probably the most dreaded task for illustrators because you love drawing and painting, but you didn't get into this to hunt down clients. However, those who are willing to put in the time will be the ones who get the jobs.

Social Media

A lot of work is given to illustrators who are consistently sharing their work on social media sites like Twitter, Facebook, and Instagram. Every art director, creative director, and editor has social media accounts and they are looking for new talent all the time. The trick is to share your work often, but never rushed or bad art. Sharing sketches can be good because a sketch isn't trying to be a polished illustration; however, don't share sloppy work just to share something for the day. Try to imagine that you're the art buyer and your job is on the line if the illustrator you hire doesn't provide excellent work.

Be creative in how you share to get more out of your efforts. Some artists share the same work five to seven times starting with a rough sketch, a finished sketch, various croppings of the finished painting, and finally a printed or framed work and possibly the art displayed at a show or held by the client or buyer. Unfortunately, it is a popularity contest out there

> **Basically, there are only two factors to getting freelance work:**
> 1. Is your work great?
> 2. Do the people who make art assignments know you exist?

Ways to find work:
- *Social Media*
- *Direct Mail*
- *SCBWI Conferences*
- *Portfolio Drop*
- *E-mail Blasts*

and you have to play the game to get noticed online. Some artists have been very successful sharing part of a project they are working on each day by creating a "story" around their creative progress.

For instance Piper Thibodeau, a Canadian illustrator, landed some great gigs (while she was still in art school!) with DreamWorks, Sesame Street, Nickelodeon, and Penguin Random House books—simply by posting her amazing work every day for a few years (She began in 2012 and is still posting a daily painting without missing a single day, as of today. (I'm writing this in 2019!) She didn't just post any work, however—she solved a daily art prompt by "sketch dailies." The act of posting each and every day no matter what and having the consistency of style, format, size, and conceptually creative ideas created a habit with her audience to "always be on the lookout" for tomorrow's offering.

Be careful about trying to maintain too many social media platforms. You are a superhero, but even superheroes have their limits. You will most likely waste time if you give just a little time to five to seven social media platforms instead of focusing your efforts on only two to four. Users tend to ignore people who only exist in "post only" mode. If you post but do not *engage* your viewers in the comment section, you will eventually teach them that leaving a comment or a like is a waste of their time. You'll be left with multiple stagnant social media accounts instead of a few vibrant sites where you create discussions and buzz about your work.

Direct Mail

Unlike social media where you have no control over who sees your work, you can choose to mail your art directly to potential clients. The most common way of doing this is by sending a post card with one of your best images printed on one side and your contact info printed on the back. A postcard is the cheapest physical piece of mail you can send. It allows you to send out plenty without breaking the bank. You don't need to say anything on the card; in fact, using tired advertising slogans such as "buy now," "available now!" or "hire me today!" will only make you look amateurish. Just let your art do the talking. If art buyers like it and have an assignment for you, they will get in touch with you.

There is a lot of information online on how to generate a mailing list, which I suggest over buying one. Developing your own list is time-consuming, but you can control who you send to and, more importantly, who *not* to waste money sending to. In general, you want to find illustrated products that you *want*. Then research the company and/or design firm or publishing house and find out who is charge of design. If you can, get the art director's name to put on the postcard; but if you can't get their name, you can simply print, "or current Art Director."

I generated my mailing list sourcing contacts from magazines in the doctor's office, book stores, Target, Walmart, and the library. I've also found many contacts online through Google searches. All of the companies you want to work for can be found online, but it will take a lot of time to generate and maintain a mailing list. Keep in mind, most artists are NOT willing to put in this kind of work, and that means that the more you do and the better you become at it, the more you are separating yourself even further from the pack. You will find obscure contacts that not many illustrators are reaching simply because you did the work and they didn't.

SCBWI Conferences

As mentioned in a previous chapter, SCBWI (Society of Children's Book Writers and Illustrators) conferences are often a great resource. Often the organizers hire art directors, agents, editors, and creative directors to speak and look at portfolios. If you want a one-on-one with one of them, it usually costs a little extra but it can be invaluable if you end up with an assignment or a book deal.

Many illustrators not only attend their own regional conferences—they also keep their eye on neighboring states' chapters. Sometimes the art director you really want to meet with is attending nearby. Lots of illustrators also attend one or both of the semi-annual conferences held in Los Angeles and New York City each year. These are huge events in comparison to the regional conferences and have more publisher contacts attending each year.

I have personally known quite a few people who owe their success to attending SCBWI conferences and meeting with the professionals attending as staff. Yes, it will cost in terms of travel expenses, time, and preparing your portfolio; but if you get your first book assignment....

Portfolio Drop

An old school method of hunting down work is to actually show up to the physical address of the company you'd like to work for and leave your portfolio with the receptionist. Back in the day, illustrators used to be able to schedule an appointment with an art director to review their portfolio in their office. Sometime in the '80's, the demand for this degree of attention overwhelmed most art directors and they changed their policies. It became common for the receptionist to not only intercept calls, but to act as gatekeeper by preventing artists from getting past the lobby. The receptionists began keeping portfolios to give to art directors to review in private...at their leisure. The artist would then pick up the portfolio the next day with hopes of a note on the work, written by the art director.

The problem with dropping your portfolio is both the time and expense, not to mention the inefficiency when compared to the previous methods I've suggested. If you travel into a city to drop a portfolio that could take half a day to get in and out—then repeat the next day to pick up—you've spent a lot of time on one potential client. However, if there are a few companies that you really, really want to work for, it could be well worth it. I just wouldn't make this your primary way of prospecting.

When I started my freelance illustration business, I dropped off three portfolios and picked three up the same day. This is because I created six physical portfolios. It was expensive but I was able to cover more ground for the money this way. You have to figure out what works for you on your budget and the time you have.

E-mail Blasts

I have never heard of any illustrator having much if any success with e-mail blasts. I only include this topic so that you don't think I overlooked it. If there's one thing that modern technology has perfected or almost perfected, it's allowing us to minimize, if not eliminate, spam in our inbox. Simply put, the art buyers you want to cold contact probably won't see your e-mail blast because they have insulated themselves from the onslaught of daily spam e-mails like yours. Unsolicited email blasts are very different than emailing to individuals who have opted in for your emails, which I will talk about in the chapter, *"Creating Your Own Brand."*

How to set up your portfolio

Your portfolio is who you are in the art world. It is a small, refined collection of your best work. The format in which you display it could be either physical, or digital—or both. The delivery method is only important to the clients you are trying to attract; in other words, how do they want to receive your portfolio? Some clients will only look at your work online, while others might prefer an in-person portfolio review or drop off.

GETTING FREELANCE WORK AFTER ART SCHOOL

I would start with an online portfolio first, since it's the cheapest and more common way clients view work. You don't need to order an expensive presentation portfolio case right out of the gate.

There are two main challenges to setting up a great portfolio and the first is fairly obvious—you need great art. The second challenge is having the guts to discard your worst pieces as you get new ones. Sounds easy, right? Except when you are starting out, you never have enough great pieces to be able to toss some of the older work...or at least that's what you think. The problem is that as you create new and better work, *all* of your previous work needs to be tossed out. The better work will excite potential clients; however, they'll only be let down when they see your older work. The only answer is to select between fifteen and twenty-five pieces of artwork for your portfolio, and when you add a new piece that is better than the rest, toss one to maintain your portfolio number.

What to include in your portfolio

Art buyers have specific needs in the assignments they give to illustrators. They have specific stories about specific problems or they have to convey details about specific concepts or products. When they look at art portfolios, they want to see subject matter that resembles their assignments. You need to include work in your portfolio that demonstrates your ability to handle many different subject matters.

I am including the following list so you can check your current portfolio for diversity of subject matter. The strategy I suggest is to create images that check multiple boxes, otherwise you would have to include too many pieces of art in your portfolio. The following list was designed for children's book illustrators, but can be easily modified for comic book, chapter book, or graphic novel work—as well as advertising/licensing portfolios. Most artists won't be able to satisfy the list for years, but it should be a goal to reach at some point.

Formats and sizes: *Spot illustrations, vignettes, full page, spreads, room for text, covers*

Color schemes: *Full color, black and white, monochrome*

Ages: *Adults, teens, children, baby*

Gender: *Girls, boys, men, women*

Race: *Asian, Indian, Hispanic, Caucasian, African*

Groups Activities: *Families, friends, classmates, co-workers*

Character Consistency: *Animals, humans, creatures*

Animals: *Anthropomorphized amphibians, mammals, fish, reptiles, insects, birds*

Creatures: *Robots, dragons, monsters, aliens, ghosts*

Vehicles: *Cars, trucks, buses, boats, planes, construction equipment, submarines, space ships*

Props: *Household items, garage, kitchen, farm, office, food, bathroom, attic, school, games, toys*

Environments: *Interiors, exteriors, modern, vintage, ancient, houses, apartments, land, sea, earth, outer space, desert, forest, tropical, arctic*

Seasons and weather: *Winter, spring, summer, fall, rain, lightning, wind, snow, fog, cold, hot*

Lighting: *Morning, noon, evening, night, spotlight, fire, ambient, on-camera, on-camera hidden, off-camera*

Surfaces: *Shiny, matte, textured, furry, translucent, rough*

Action: *Falling, breaking, sliding, moving fast, running, jumping, flying, rolling, skidding*

Emotion: *Anger, excitement, happiness, sadness, fear, confidence, curiosity, love, sleeping, pain*

Scale: *Huge objects, tiny objects*

Camera Angles: *Establishing, close ups, medium, distant, high angle, low angle, profile, dynamic, POV.*

Complex Images: *Multiple figures, multiple objects*

Your Website

We've talked about your portfolio, but we haven't addressed your website in general. The presentation of your online portfolio is as important as the quality of your artwork. The visual design and navigation will either enhance or detract from your work. If you take the best artwork from the best artist and place it on a badly-designed website, it won't perform as well as slightly-lesser art on a beautifully-designed site. I suggest using a service like Squarespace, because it's easy to use, easy to modify, and the templates Squarespace provides are designed by pros. There really isn't a good excuse to have a poorly-designed site anymore.

What should you share on your website? Well, the best place to start is to look at twenty of the top artists' websites that are doing the kind of work you want to do. If you want to be a gallery artist, you should be looking at gallery artists' websites. If you want to become a children's book illustrator, look at twenty of the top children's book illustrators' websites. Comic book artists? You get the picture.

There are some constants that cross over for artists working in just about every genre, and the following list should probably be included on your site:

1. **Portfolio** *The headings could be displayed as Work, Art, Paintings, Drawings, etc.*
2. **Bio** *Your clients want to know about you, so tell them a few interesting anecdotes that will make you more interesting to your clients. And please include your portrait.*
3. **Shop** *This could also be called "Store" or "Buy" or "For Sale." When you start out, you might not have anything to sell but this is an easy way to generate more income when you are ready.*
4. **Contact** *Obviously, you want to be contacted by art buyers, so display your email address or an email capture.*

After you have been at this awhile, you might want to add the following:

1. **Blog**
2. **Client list**
3. **Schedule of appearances**
4. **List of shows** you've been in and will be in
5. **YouTube channel**

The presentation of your online portfolio is as important as the quality of your artwork.

If we imagine your marketing efforts as a wheel, your portfolio should be the "hub" of the wheel. The spokes are represented by each individual action you take that draws attention to your work. Spokes could include:

- Making a YouTube video about your work or process
- Mailing postcards
- Making social media posts
- Giving a talk
- Teaching a class
- Selling your work at a festival or convention, etc.

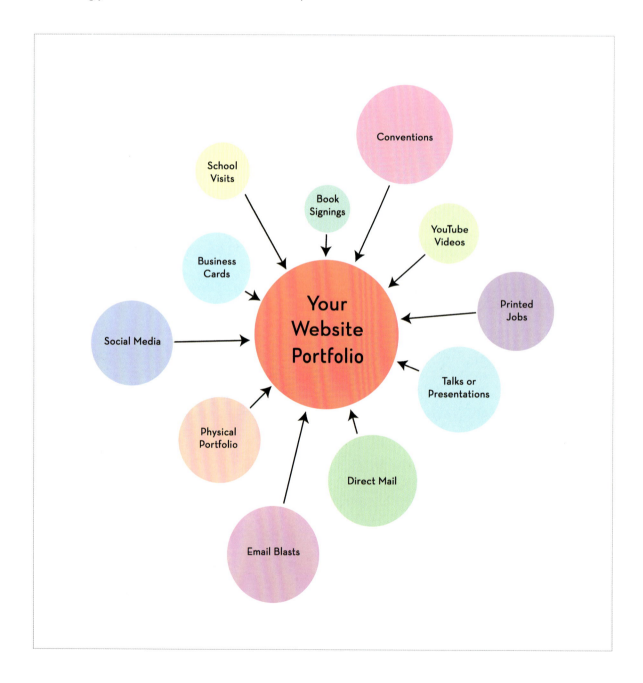

Each of your spokes need to lead to the "hub"—or your portfolio. All of the activities you do with your work should also push or promote your website because your website should be able to convert potential art buyers. If your website is set up well, it should be the best way to display your work for potential clients.

How do I get a rep?

Before I answer how to get one, let me first ask if you are you ready for a rep? Relationships tend to thrive when the value proposition from each side is closer to equal. Person A has this valuable thing that person B needs, and person B has a valuable thing that person A needs. If your art isn't as good as the current stable of artists a rep has, then that puts you in a much lower bargaining position. Reps have been known to take advantage of artists on the lower end of their talent scale. To prevent this, you need to make sure your value is as high as possible.

> All of the activities you do with your work should also push or promote your website because your website should be able to convert potential art buyers.

One way a rep can "take advantage of you" is to sign you as a backup artist, in case his or her main artists are too busy to accept an assignment. She won't tell you that you're being signed as a second, third, or even fourth-string illustrator—you just won't get much, if any, work. The rep doesn't care if you quit, because it didn't cost much to sign you in the first place.

Reps also do not usually take on talent right out of school. An artist representative wants to know that you are serious about the business of illustration, which means they want to see that you have already started your freelance practice. They want to see that you have already worked with clients and that you have the portfolio to reflect that. They want to know that you have learned the hard work of marketing your own work—mostly because they want you to really value what they will be doing for you. After all, it's both time-consuming and risky if you don't know how to treat clients and deliver great work on time, in proper formats.

Ok, so you've been out of school for a year or two and have been working hard looking for and finding a few clients here and there and your work is great! So how do you find a rep? Well the good news is that they are easy to find. All of the artist representatives have websites and can be found through a simple Google search.

My advice is to search these keywords in various combinations:
Artist, rep, representative, children's, book, publishing, illustration, editorial, advertising.

When you bring up a list of sites, visit them individually and copy their contact info. If you are already sending out postcards of your work to clients, simply add ten to twenty reps to your mailings. If your work is great, at least one of them will eventually contact you.

Reps might also find you from your social media efforts, so you might not ever really have to search out a rep.

How do I know if the terms of the rep contract are good?

Great! You've been approached by a rep and they have expressed interest in representing you, but how do you know if their terms are standard or an over-reach? In my opinion, almost every rep contract has overreaching demands that do not work in the artist's favor. They will want all of your work to run through them so they get a percentage. Some will allow you to retain "house accounts" (clients you had before you signed with them) while others will not. They will want to take 30-35% of the commissions they negotiate for you, which is high in my opinion. Industry standard was historically 25% and the Internet should have made it cheaper for reps to run their business.

Some reps want you to stay with them for six months after you sever the contract plus one month for every year you were together. This means that if you were under contract for 6 years and you decided it wasn't working for you and you asked to get out, you would have to stay for another year. You would be in breach of contract if you began prospecting for work on your own without turning over new clients to your rep. I understand why a rep would want you to agree to this term because it protects them and hurts you, but I have no idea why illustrators regularly sign under these conditions.

Everything is negotiable. Remember that—EVERYTHING is negotiable. You do not have to agree to all of the terms in the contract. You can cross out or discuss with the rep certain parts of the agreement that you do not like. If the rep feels that they are in a stronger bargaining position, they might tell you that they won't represent you if you do not sign the entire contract as is. In the end, it's going to be up to you to decide what you're willing and not willing to live with.

> In my opinion, almost every rep contract has overreaching demands that do *not* work in the artist's favor.

Vetting a rep

There is one good way to vet a rep. Before I share the method, let me share a few rep nightmares—I've known of three illustrators who really felt they got the raw end of the deal with their reps.

The first was a teacher and friend of mine who had to endure little-to-no work for about a year-and-a-half, while his rep funneled his projects—including work which was specifically requested by the client—to other illustrators. The day he told his rep that he wanted to dissolve the contract, she informed him that his contract stated that he could not prospect for new clients until the "six month plus one month for every year they were together" waiting period was up—totaling about a year-and-a-half! It crippled his family finances for the duration.

Another friend found out that his rep was funneling his projects to other illustrators in the group, simply because his rep wanted to keep the "stable of artists" happy. So, when a client requested my friend, his rep sometimes told the client he couldn't take the work because he was booked...when he wasn't.

But here's the coup de grâce: I have a friend who was with a rep that stole money from all of her talent for a year! The rep had premeditatedly funded her illegal retirement package by keeping her artists' share of the money that they earned on assignments. Beyond pure evil, this Mephistopheles began telling artists that their clients were late to pay; then she would tell them that she was sending their clients threatening letters to pay up. As time went by, she kept feeding them more work, knowing full well she was going to pocket all the money. What were the artists supposed to do? They needed work to stay alive and she was very good at convincing them to keep working, as all the money would eventually landslide into their mailboxes. Month by month, the artists slaved away as she worked extra hard to load them up with work. Eventually, she would say that she got checks from their clients but since they were for the wrong amounts, she had to send them back, requesting new checks. Towards the end, she would tell them that she had just received the check and would forward their percentages due, but of course she never sent anything. She would then blame the postal service for losing the check, letting them know she would go through the cancellation and re-issuing process. Of course, "this is going to take a little more time."

Eventually, "she-devil" moved to another country, never to be heard from again. The artists began contacting each other, comparing notes, trying to unravel the mystery. By then, it was too late—she had absconded with well over $1,000,000 of their hard-earned money!

So, what can you do to protect yourself? It's quite simple—ask any rep that is interested in representing you to give you contact info for his or her artists. If they refuse, they will give you a reason that probably won't pass the smell test. I wouldn't sign with a rep that won't let you talk to their group. I would just assume that they are planning a LONG vacation.

Maybe I don't even want a rep?

There are definitely some upsides and downsides to having a rep and many feel that the benefits outweigh the negatives. Conversely, there are many artists who won't have a rep. Let's look at some of the pros and cons:

Pros

- *More time to create rather than prospect for clients*
- *Higher-paying jobs because reps negotiate for higher fees*
- *Better jobs with bigger companies*
- *Rep collects on late-paying clients*
- *Rep invoices clients*
- *Rep reviews your contracts with clients*
- *Professional industry advice on your career*
- *Rep maintains the website and marketing*

Cons

- *Waits and delays for jobs*
- *You may earn the same fees on some jobs as you would have earned on your own*
- *Delay in getting paid until after your rep has been paid*
- *You may rely too heavily on your rep and let your business atrophy*
- *25–35% of your income goes to your rep*
- *Jobs come in for you but are diverted to another artist*
- *Rep turns down jobs (that you never heard about) that he/she thought were too small*
- *Not hearing direct feedback from the client*
- *Miscommunication on assignment details due to one more person in the loop*
- *Having to stay with a rep for months after you've fired them, while they divert your projects to other talent*

What is the difference between a rep and an agent?

Simply put, a rep customarily represents illustrators exclusively while an agent usually represents *writers* exclusively. There are some agents who also represent illustrators but usually only if they are also writing their own stories. Agents typically charge 10-15% which begs the question: Why do reps charge so much—25-35%—for doing the same amount of work? I've never heard a good answer to this question other than, historically, reps used to have to pay more to create and send portfolios of work which was much more expensive than dropping a manuscript in the mail. But nowadays, almost all images are managed on the rep's website; therefore, costs *should* have decreased, and subsequently the rep's commission percentage along with it.

My work is great and I have a rep but I'm not getting enough work...

I touched on this in the previous chapter, but it is a very common and constant question for beginning and intermediate artists. You've done everything right and yet no one is offering you assignment work, *or* the work trickles in so slowly you can't pay all of your bills. The simple fact is that there are and always have been more qualified illustrators than assignments. You could be on the verge of getting assignments that could change everything; but through bad luck, these assignments are going to other artists. Many times, art buyers select multiple illustrators for one project and then through debate, choose *one* over all the others. The sad part is that those who did not win the contract usually never know they were even in the running.

I suspect that many artists have quit right when they were about to catch their first break without ever knowing it. In the meantime, while you're waiting for that magical email, you should really work on your own projects. Not only can you self-publish your work to earn money, your project can also serve as a marketing tool to land assignments. I know this because I know many artists who have launched their own careers with their own creations.

> I know many artists who have launched their own careers with their own creations. Artists have never had as much power as they do today. The challenge for you is to recognize the opportunities and seize them.

GETTING FREELANCE WORK AFTER ART SCHOOL

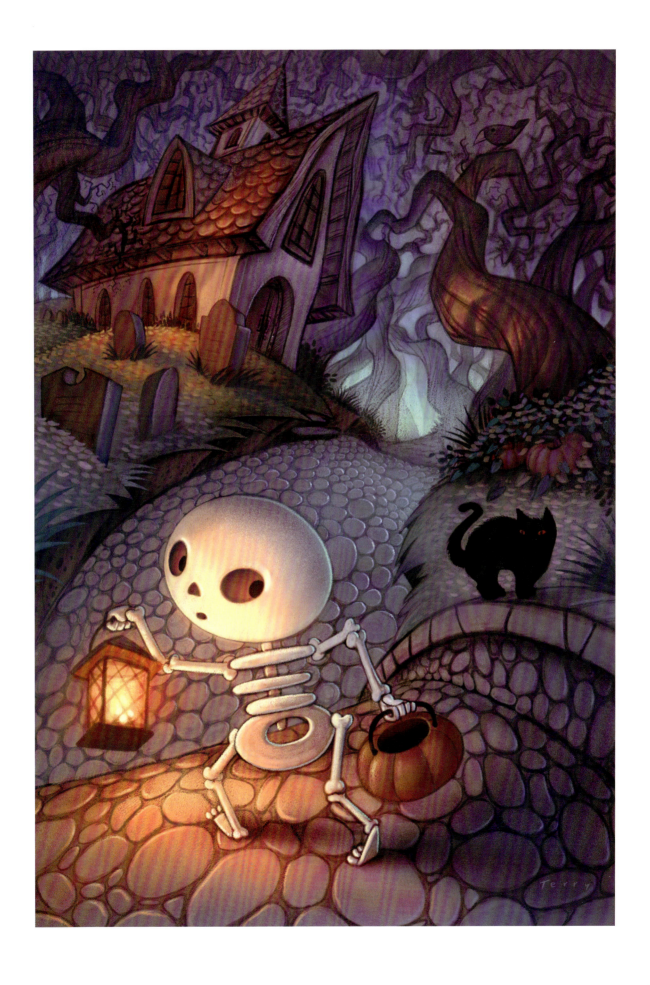

Artists have never had as much power as they do today. The challenge for you is to recognize the opportunities and seize them. Historically, artists have had to have their work purchased and published by sponsors or foundations, benefactors, and promoters—gatekeepers, in other words. Not too long ago, before the internet, musicians had to have the backing of a record label; actors had to be chosen by studios; dancers by companies; and yes, writers and illustrators by publishers.

Today, musicians can produce professional recordings for free or very inexpensively in their home with online recording studios, instead of spending thousands of dollars for live studio time (as it was in the 1970s!). Actors and commentators can now produce their own shows directly on YouTube and many have been hired by studios due to the exposure they've created.

Likewise, authors and illustrators have created books, magazines, graphic novels, novels, art books, and comics using page-layout software, like InDesign. These artists have had great commercial success on their own and have kept much higher percentages of the profits. Amazon and other popular websites facilitate transactions and worldwide distribution that never existed only a few decades ago. The gold, however, is the exposure these artists have received from their own self-published projects and the careers they have launched as a result.

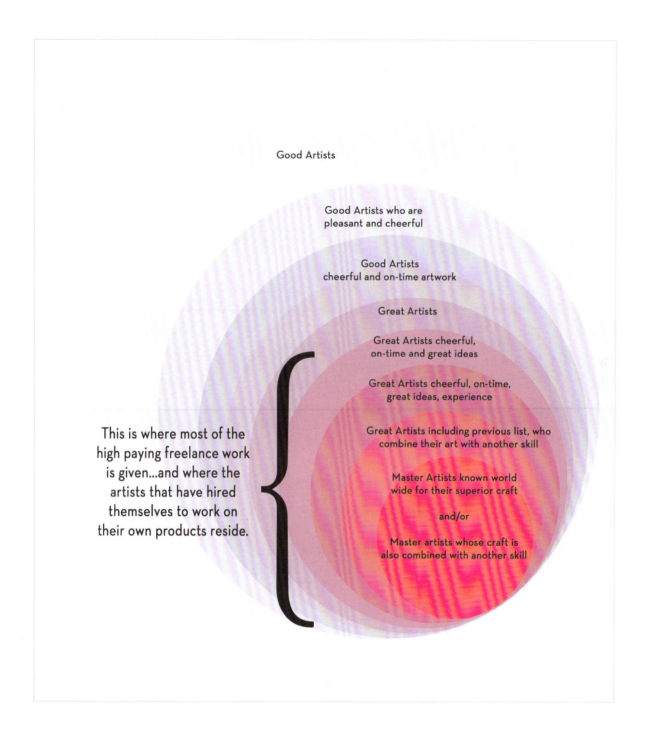

Great artists began as good artists. Good artists who really want to get work must also be easy to work with if they want clients to take a chance on them. Good artists should be especially accommodating and work to send in sketches and final art early and at least on-time. As you become a great artist you should be looking at ways of becoming even greater. Suggesting better concepts and ideas will set you apart from the rest. Master artists have realized that there is no such thing as "arriving"—they understand that the pursuit is never over—that growth is and should be a constant through the life of an artist.

GETTING FREELANCE WORK AFTER ART SCHOOL

"Describing yourself as creator—or creative—or artist—allows you more mental flexibility when describing what you do, and what you are capable of."

CREATING YOUR OWN BRAND

What is a brand?

A brand is a personal style with identifying features that make it unique to a specific product or line of products. Artists often generate a personal style, but many never create their own line of products.

For instance, I developed a cross hatching style with color overlays to define my "Little Heroes" line of characters. I've also used this style in my "Bonaparte" children's books for Random House. I use a tight parallel rhythmic line stroke with a digital pencil in Procreate (an iPad app), to get this effect. I use it on all the characters in my pop culture characters, which creates continuity. These characters become branded with my personal style. To further "brand" these characters and join them as one product line, they are all printed at the same size, on the same paper, with the same white background.

My fan art book, "Little", was intentionally designed with my brand in mind—the solo figures, white backgrounds—even my cross hatching was used as a design element on the book's endsheets and section separator pages.

82 **WILL TERRY** *What They Don't Teach in Art School*

CREATING YOUR OWN BRAND

Your brand should always be apparent and consistent. This consistency helps potential customers easily comprehend what they can expect from me, and it makes me instantly recognizable when they see my booth at shows *(see facing)*.

Another example of an artist who has created his own brand is Jake Parker. Jake began his career in animation working for Reel FX and Blue Sky Studios, where he sharpened his drawing and design skills. He leveraged that success into creating his own comic book series, Missile Mouse, which landed him children's book deals with major publishers.

He then created the uber-popular "Inktober" challenge and "Art Drop Day."

As co-founder of SVSLearn.com along with yours truly, he also launched the 3 POINT PERSPECTIVE podcast, which has become a favorite among animators and illustrators. And let's not forget that he started "Art Drop Club" with Aaron Painter. What does all of this have to do with his brand? Well, because of his involvement in these high-profile endeavors, he has extreme reach on social media to market his online shop where he sells books, stickers, prints, posters, comics, originals, and phone cases...and his sales are impressive.

© Jake Parker, used with permission.

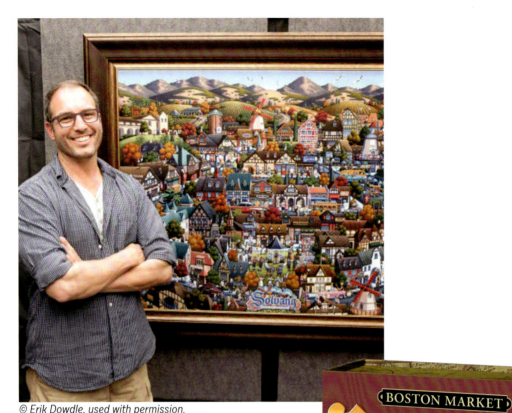

© Erik Dowdle, used with permission.

"**Eric Dowdle's** unique style in painting folk art first developed when he began painting two-dimensional images of villages and landscapes. He created specific city replicas in his folk art style—places like San Francisco, Chicago, Austin, and many other cities.

Later, he had a unique idea for marketing his folk art paintings—to print them as puzzles. These brainteasers have been around for how long? Forever. Anyway, it was a brilliantly simple plan—each city had gift shops, and tourists might want to purchase a unique puzzle of the city they had visited. It worked, and today Dowdle Folk Art is a prominent brand in both the art and puzzle industry."

vonda@dowdlefolkart.com

Craftsman vs creator

If you went to art school or if you went through a similar online art program, you were mostly taught to think of yourself as a: graphic designer, illustrator, animator, fine artist, sculptor, photographer, painter, print maker, etc. After most of the required foundational programs are completed, all artists split into separate camps reflecting one of these labels. I believe this changed something in our way of thinking. As you mature as an artist, you start to see glaring similarities between every discipline in the arts, and even similarities with sports as a creative endeavor. When you are in an art school program, you are separated into your chosen discipline and primarily focus on the differences between your camp and the other camps. We also tend to define ourselves by the label we were given: illustrator, animator, painter, etc.

This is a limiting way to think about yourself, because you are capable of producing many more projects outside of your label. Maybe you can't animate if you're an illustrator but it wouldn't take much instruction for you to connect the dots. So, you haven't had all of the classes? Big deal—you have learned many of the same principles that the students in those other classes learned. The truth is that once you've mastered one, it should take only a fraction of time to learn others.

Your art school program, thankfully, was/is designed to help you become a master at one discipline. If you take what you learn in a four-year program or combination of online schools and apply hard work, you can become a master craftsman in your particular discipline years down the road. When you become a master, you can compete for work with other master artists working in your field. This is a hard but viable way to seek commercial success.

There is however, another way, for us to think of ourselves—as what I call "creators" or simply "artists."

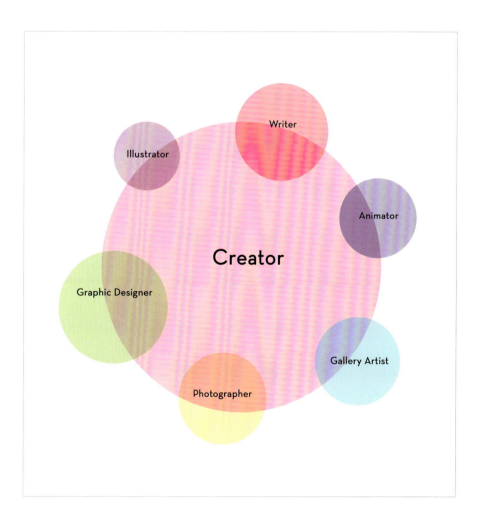

WILL TERRY *What They Don't Teach in Art School*

Describing yourself as creator or creative or artist allows you more mental flexibility when describing what you do and what you are capable of. When we put defined labels on ourselves, we tend to limit our capacity, or abilities, and the projects we think we can accomplish. When we broaden our description, we are free to think of ourselves as much more.

When you allow yourself to believe you can do more, you allow yourself to begin projects that will take you out of your comfort zone and will combine more than one area of expertise. So you aren't as great at a second area just yet? Do you realize how many successful projects have been launched where the artist or creator wasn't great at one or more of the skills he or she needed?

For example, Scott Adams has always maintained that he wasn't much of a writer nor cartoonist but when he combined the two, something magical happened and his Dilbert cartoon became a multi-million dollar entity. Mo Willems was a writer for Nickelodeon, but he never had illustration training and yet somehow, he was brave enough to put on his illustrator boots and become not only a New York Times bestselling author/illustrator—he's also received the Caldecott Honor award. And then there's Mathew Inman who didn't go to school for writing or illustrating, but used his creativity to start a web comic called "The Oatmeal." Not only did he sell over $500,000/year from his online shop, he created a card game that raised $8.7 million on Kickstarter.

The craftsman has to "out-craft" his or her competitors, which is doable; but it often means decades of dedication to improving one specific skill. The creator can create a product without necessarily mastering all skills needed to produce a product that has mass appeal. There are a lot of successful entrepreneurs walking this earth that are less qualified than you in one or more of the skills they employ to make money.

> **Describing yourself as creator or creative or artist allows you more mental flexibility when describing what you do and what you are capable of.**

How can I develop my own brand?

I believe your brand begins with your personal style, which I talked about in the chapter *"Becoming a Master Artist."* Because you are unique in your experiences and the way you view and interpret the world you are in a unique position to create a brand.

Think of a brand as a flavor, sound, smell, look, or feel. Since this book is mostly targeting visual artists we are mostly talking about the look of your art. Specifically, what key characteristics link your work– what are identifiable qualities of your work? In your early days as an artist your work will feel dis-jointed and mostly unrelated. The longer you work on your art the more cohesive your pieces will become (this is your style). I'm going to suggest that you think of your work as a brand over time.

As you get better and better at creating art, you should think about the key identifiable characteristics that are unique to you—or the sum of the key features that are unique to you. Leaning into these key features or emphasizing them will further "brand" your art and make it feel original to viewers. Product manufacturers are constantly looking for ways to differentiate themselves from their competition, and so should you.

CREATING YOUR OWN BRAND

After you create a body of consistent work with a consistent style, it's time to print your work on various products. In creating your own brand you will also need to think about graphic design.

Your art will feel very different depending on the way you apply it to products. Do you use full bleeds? Lots of white space? Do you give it a retro feel with a heavy dot pattern? Do you combine it with type? If so, what font(s)? Do you print it heavy and bold or very light? Do you use an accent color that matches your art?

You will need to make decisions for your brand that will give your consumers the same or similar feeling whenever they see your work.

Perhaps you start with prints since they are one of the cheapest, easiest, most understood products you can produce. Get your feet wet a little bit at a time. Maybe you experiment with a matching game or a deck of face cards with your art. Over time, you will develop a product line; more importantly, you will spend time learning valuable lessons in product creation and development. When you think about your brand, you will inevitably think about other ideas and possibilities or products you can create.

Some of you are asking, "Yeah, but I'm just an artist, how do I get the money to fund a product or line of products?" Have I got good news for you! Keep reading.

Marketing your brand

Modern marketing is really as simple as identifying your audience and presenting them with your project/ product and showing them how to get it. Easier said than done but the following methods have proven themselves again and again. Keep in mind that new ways to identify your audience and share your products are being discovered and evolving all the time. Don't be afraid to pioneer your own methods because often the freshest marketing ideas attract the most attention.

> You will need to make decisions for your brand that will give your consumers the same or similar feeling whenever they see your work.

> In your early days as an artist your work will feel dis-jointed and mostly unrelated. The longer you work on your art the more cohesive your pieces will become (this is your style). I'm going to suggest that you think of your work as a brand over time.

Email gold

A popular principle in marketing niche products is that you need to find your 1000 true fans. What are "true fans"? Well, they are not people that like your work or know about you or even people who have bought your work. True fans are people who want and buy just about everything you produce! Think about fans who follow bands around the world to attend their concerts.

Finding your 1000 true fans can be a lifelong pursuit but it's definitely possible. As you grow your list from 10 to 50 and then to 100, you are going to need to be able to contact them to make future announcements on future products you are offering.

> True fans are people who want and buy just about everything you produce!

CREATING YOUR OWN BRAND

Collecting their emails is vital for both of you.

Your website should have an email capture app that allows your fans to opt in for your announcements. Most of the people that give you their email addresses will not be your true fans but many will help you spread your art or will buy something now and then. Your true fans however, will join your list over time and will support you as you gain in popularity.

Your email list is pure gold, because these people want to know about your next project so they can buy it. In marketing, there is an acronym—CAC or *customer acquisition cost*—which is the money you spend, on average, to find a new customer. Your email list will always have the lowest CAC, because your customers found you and asked you to sell them your future work—for free. It didn't cost you anything.

Free for email

One way to build your email list is to give something away for free to those who sign up or fill in the email capture on your website. If you give away a physical product like a greeting card, comic, or game, you will not only have to pay for the product but also the shipping costs—or charge for the shipping in which case your free giveaway isn't actually free. The most cost effective free products are digital. Successful artists give away a chapter or two of their comic or graphic novel, screen savers, posters, printable greeting cards, advice, knowledge, how-to instructions, etc.

Whatever you can think of that will be valuable to someone else and that can be delivered digitally can be a great incentive for someone to give you their email address. This is a numbers game—the more

> Your email list is pure gold, because these people want to know about your next project so they can buy it.

emails you have that are self qualified, (which means they signed up because they love what you do), the more sales you will generate from paid content on your site later.

Free marketing on social media

There are entire books dedicated to marketing on social media, so I'm going to cover a lot very quickly.

First, you need to understand the psychology behind social media and why it's become the number one way we communicate with people outside our home. It's a way we connect ourselves to the most important people in our lives from family and friends to those we don't know personally like influencers, celebrities, and producers. You are probably not an "influencer" or celebrity, but if you're looking to market your products using social media you are a producer.

People want to follow the producers of content or products they enjoy, like, love, and/or want.

An artist gains followers because the artist is sharing content that is interesting. If the content is low quality or boring the artist is going to struggle to gain followers. If the artist improves their quality of content they will gain followers over time. If the artist changes the type of content or lowers the quality of content the artist will lose followers. In a game of numbers its always important to work to gain followers.

Understanding this will help you to understand that sharing content that is very different from the normal content you share is risky. You can easily lose followers if you share someone's work, project, or product that's very different or even offensive to your audience. This is why it's often regarded as an over-reach to ask someone to share your project on their social media accounts. It's hard to tell your friend that you're worried their content will cause a certain level of attrition from your followers if you share it. It's better that you don't ask your friends to share your project and then you can more easily turn them down if they ask.

You should however share other people's amazing content if it's in line with what you normally share. For example, if you regularly share dark charcoal drawings of monsters and you see one of your favorite artist's monster drawings that knocks your socks off, why not share it? You connect yourself to them and they love the extra boost while giving your followers more of what they come to you for. It's win-win and it's a more efficient way of building your following. Most artists cannot come up with daily or even every other day content and that's where sharing other's amazing work can boost your followers faster.

> **Understand the psychology.** *People want to follow the producers of content or products they enjoy, like, love, and/or want.*
>
> **Improve your content, increase your followers.**
>
> **Let people consume the gifts you create for free.** *You need to know that your social media should be mostly about giving.*
>
> **Enjoy sharing on social media** *or you won't be able to keep it up for the years it takes to build these platforms of communication.*

You can easily lose followers if you share someone's work, project, or product that's very different or even offensive to your audience.

Second, you need to know that your social media should be mostly about giving. Most of the year you should be focused on giving away your art on your social media accounts letting people consume the gifts you create for free. You are giving because artists are great at giving and here's the key: when the time is right you're going to ask. Gary Vaynerchuk calls it "jab, jab, jab, punch" meaning that most of what you are going to be doing is small giving or jabs (soft punches) so that you can finally punch– asking, announcing, offering, or calling to action on a product you are releasing.

It's paramount that you enjoy sharing on social media or you won't be able to keep it up for the years it takes to build these platforms of communication. The technology we have called social media is so unbelievable compared to the telephone, tv, and radio of yesterday. The challenge you have is to see the opportunities for what they are. If you ignore this technology because you think it's negative, or a time waste, or you are an introvert and can't be expected to participate you will consign yourself to irrelevance as an artist. It's imperative that you learn how to make at least one of these platforms work for you.

If you don't like making videos do NOT start a YouTube channel. If you love making videos, YouTube might be perfect for you. If you don't like engaging with people on Instagram or Facebook just post your work and let people enjoy it. If you like short

witty conversations you might find Twitter to be your playground. There's nothing like being able to have thousands of followers waiting to hear about your product—but too often, artists wait until their product is finished to think about starting a social media account. Don't let this be you.

Paid marketing on social media

If you are one of those who have decided to sit out on social media and you are ready to launch your product you can pay for advertising on social media…but it's going to cost you. It's much cheaper to share your products with your followers but you can put your products in front of potential buyers if you have money to gamble with. The applications you can use on Facebook, Instagram, YouTube, etc. are ever-changing. There are always new ways to create and share paid ads on these platforms, so I'm not going to provide specific information on how to buy ads.

The more important information is to know that you must have a product that when sold can gain $3 for every $1 spent on ads—or better. If you cannot regain $3 of revenue for every $1 spent on ads, your product or ads are not "working".

For example: Webvan was a dot com business started in the early 2000s in San Francisco. Webvan delivered groceries from stores to consumers in their homes. They spent over one billion dollars buying delivery vans and warehouses only to find out that people don't want their groceries delivered for the price they were offering. At its peak in 2000, Webvan had $178.5 million in sales but it also had $525.4 million in expenses.

Just because you can pay for ads and generate sales doesn't mean you have a profitable product.

> Too often, artists wait until their product is finished to think about starting a social media account. Don't let this be you.

Content marketing

I don't want to spend a lot of time on this one but quite simply it's the idea that if you provide quality information (content) online, the Google algorithms can put your website, blog, or video at the top of searches. If people can find your content then it's not too hard to get some of them to visit your website. If you talk about your website in the content now and then—even better.

Example: I am planning to market a board game I'm working on. A year or two before launching it I started a blog about the best board games, or the best indie board games, or maybe how to play test your board game or how to create a great game—the more focused the better. In my blog articles now and then I mention the board game I'm working on and as I build my audience and as they interact with my blog - they become intrigued by my story. My audience is looking forward to the day I launch my product for sale because they have been invested long before I launch. I attracted them with content marketing.

Content marketing is a great way to drive internet traffic to your website by offering valuable information for free on your website.

> Content marketing is a great way to drive internet traffic to your website by offering valuable information for free on your website.

Free product to sell merchandise

Many artists have found that if they give away their core product for free, they can leverage that product to sell ancillary products or merchandise. If an artist creates a webcomic or an advice channel, or a blog, or perhaps they give away their webcomic, advice, or instruction for free. Then they can sell merchandise that goes along with their core product that their fans want to collect or use.

The trick is to create enough value to gain followers of your work. Easier said than done? Sure, but you are giving it away for free so getting eyes on your work is much easier than if your work is behind a paywall. If you look at any of the many popular free web comics (just Google "free web comics") there's a reason that many of them have many thousands if not hundreds of thousands of readers—the work is excellent and it's free! When I say the work is excellent, I mean that the product combination of art and writing is valuable to a certain demographic.

CREATING YOUR OWN BRAND

Explore the popular free web comics and you will almost always find merchandise for sale on the site and that's how the artist is using their core product as a lure to hook consumers for free and some of them will have to have that coffee mug or T-shirt. Giving away your product for free is going to feel wrong at first. You're going to ask yourself why you're giving it away and how you it will ever be worth it? You better be doing it because you love it because that's all you will be getting in the beginning as you build your audience. Over time as you gain readers you will be able to offer them paid products that a fraction will want and be willing to buy. The larger the readership, the more money you can make selling merchandise.

Creating scarcity

Another way to create buzz and sales is to create a product in a limited quantity. The idea is that if you have an unlimited supply of product, consumers don't have any urgency or need to act. Likewise you can tap into the "fear of loss" most humans have by letting them know that when your supply runs out there will be no more. If customers don't act now, they might miss out.

This can work for you to generate sales quickly but it's also a double edged sword. If you have a really popular product you cannot ethically make more of them when they sell out. Boutique toy companies often use this marketing strategy by promoting and releasing limited edition toys at shows. There's often a "feeding

CREATING YOUR OWN BRAND

frenzy" atmosphere when the doors open and customers run through the show to get to their favorite toy company booth to line up for the chance to get as many of the limited toys as they are allowed to purchase. Often these buyers re-sell the limited edition toys online to the highest bidder.

Collectors want to know that they have something special—something that you can't get anymore. Creating limited editions can give you more to talk about on your platforms and entice buyers to buy today.

Keep the sold out items on your website with a "sold out" label over them so that visitors will see that if they don't act now they might miss out forever.

Working with a marketing person

I have learned my limitations when it comes to marketing my own art and products. I've learned a lot but there are specialty niche areas of marketing that constantly change as new technologies and platforms become available. Facebook for instance is constantly updating or releasing new apps for marketers. These are apps that run behind the scenes—apps that users rarely know anything about.

When these new options become available there are early adopters willing to give them a try and willing to experiment. I've found that as I'm focused on creating my products I just don't have time to tinker with all the options available nor do I want to. You are better off spending your time on things you enjoy

> Keep the sold out items on your website with a "sold out" label over them so that visitors will see that if they don't act now they might miss out forever.

because it will show in your work. If you dread researching, reading about, taking tutorials, tinkering, and troubleshooting software options on social media it will likewise show—in your failures.

If you haven't spent four years in a marketing or entrepreneurial major in college you probably lack a lot of the theory and knowledge about modern marketing. If you don't know what CPC, CPL, CPM, CRM, CTA, CTR, CR, CRO, CX/UX, GDD, BR, KPI, SEO, PR, RFP, SAAS, and SMM means, don't worry—someone else does and they not only love knowing, they want great products to be able to market.

I would much rather partner with someone who loves doing the aforementioned than tearing my hair out struggling to keep all the booty. Giving up a percentage of profits (partnering up) can yield much higher gross returns on sales because both of you are doing what you love. Why partner instead of paying a marketing person? If you have the cash to pay a marketer that might be a great option so you can retain full ownership of your product/company. But there are no guarantees the marketer you pay will successfully sell your product—but they will take your money. I prefer to partner so that my marketer has "skin in the game"—in other words, if I don't get paid, my marketer doesn't get paid either.

Downsides to partnerships are mainly arguments over product and marketing decisions and potentially unscrupulous business decisions. I've found that I'm good at judging character long before I sign a partnership agreement and knock on wood—so far so good! Some may say that giving up a percentage of your business is a downside but I choose to see it as a win-win. I want my partner to become a millionaire because guess what? That's right—I do too.

How can you find a marketing person willing to partner with you and work for free in the beginning? This is as you probably guessed—much easier said than done. The better your product however and the more advanced you are in your career the easier it is. My marketing partner for this book jumped at the chance to work with me on it. That wouldn't have happened in the beginning of my career but I guarantee you that if you have a product that a marketer thinks they can easily sell—they will lick their chops to be able to work on selling it for you.

> **You are better off spending your time on things you enjoy because it will show in your work. If you dread researching, reading about, taking tutorials, tinkering, and troubleshooting software options on social media it will likewise show—in your failures.**

CREATING YOUR OWN BRAND

How do you determine what percentage to offer? This is a very tricky part. Give away too much and you will resent your partner as you feel like they are reaping more than the value they provided. Underpay your marketer and you'll often find them working on someone else's project or quitting yours. I've worked in 50/50 partnerships when it felt right—30/70 partnerships, and 20/80 partnerships. If you really want to protect yourself, you can opt to bonus your marketing person rather than draw up an operating agreement listing them as part owner (percentage). Some marketers will go for this while others will insist on ownership.

You can create a simple schedule of profit sharing based on quarterly sales. **For example:** Sally is going to become your marketing partner but you are not going to give her a percentage of your business—you are going to give her guaranteed quarterly profit percentages. So let's say you agree to pay Sally 10% of sales if she sells 500 units in a quarter. You also agree to pay her 20% of sales from 501-1000 units

and 30% on 1001-1500 units, and so on. The math can get a little complicated but not really—the more she sells in a quarter, the more she can earn for herself. The idea is to incentivize her to sell more and more—to go beyond what your expectations are. The more she makes, the more you make.

You can make much more money giving away a good chunk of your profits to a marketing person who is capable, innovative, and hard working, than trying to wear all the hats yourself. So you can make $50k by yourself but with a 50% partner your company grosses $200k? As you try to scale your business you will run into challenges that are often solved by working with another person or a team. A winning mindset is to think in abundance rather than hoarding what money is coming in. If you are creating a great product, it's eventually going to take a team to share it with the world.

> You can make much more money giving away a good chunk of your profits to a marketing person who is capable, innovative, and hard working, than trying to wear all the hats yourself.

Crowdfunding

I don't think there's a single person on this planet that hasn't heard of companies like Kickstarter or Indiegogo. I'm only including this section of the book because it deserves mention. However, there are so many strategies, techniques, and methods needed to run a successful crowdfunding campaign, it would require its own book—and there are already good ones out there.

Historically, if you had an idea for a product and wanted to produce and market it you were limited by the amount of money you had or the amount of money you could sweet talk out of potential investors. Then came the internet and crowdfunding sites—Kickstarter being the most popular.

In a nutshell, crowdfunding works like this: anyone can conceive of a product, describe it on a crowdfunding platform with video, text, images, and graphics. Then they "launch their campaign" and pre-sell their product before it is created, eliminating the need to produce an unproven product at great expense. Their campaign usually runs for about a 30 day duration where they take orders, and collect money from sales before they pay for printing, sculpting, 3-d printing, manufacturing, etc. When the campaign ends, the crowdfunding site transfers the money they raised (minus the site's small percentage) to their bank account. They are then obligated to pay expenses related to creating the product and fulfilling their promise by shipping their product to customers.

There has never been a better time to be alive as an artist with ambition! The limits have evaporated and the opportunities have been magnified by technology. You're only limited by your own imagination and determination.

105

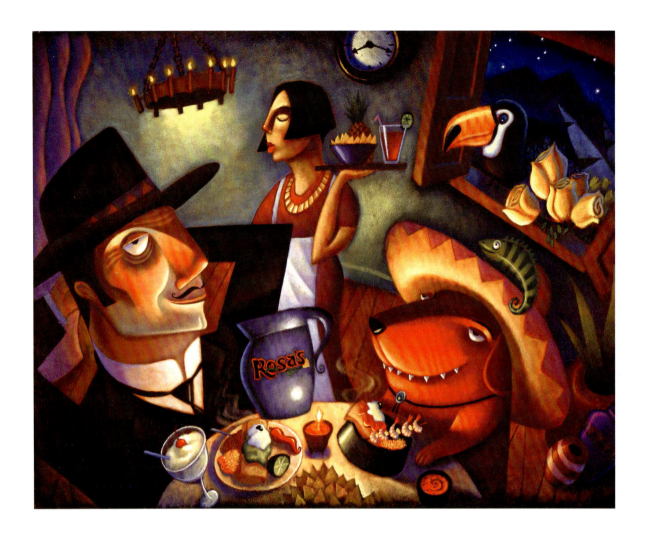

Funding companies

Funding companies are 3rd party entities that work with crowdfunding websites to boost the sales for individuals or companies. Some refer to them as "digital wallets". If you have a crowdfunding campaign that is fully funded and growing in sales, funding companies may contact you or you may contact them to sign a contract whereby they spend their own money to market your product during your campaign.

Here's how it works: You are selling a game or book and your campaign is launched on a platform like Kickstarter and you've reached your funding goal. Often it's right after you achieve funding which should be in the first day or so that your campaign has launched. You have proven that there is a market for your project and the funding company thinks that they can make money off your project while making you even more money than you would have made. Because you've funded in the first few days there's plenty of time for the funding company to make Facebook/Instagram ads to target the kinds of customers you've already found in your campaign.

The funding company will ask you for an amount of money they can use to test the ads they made for your project. The test money varies from company to company and is definitely negotiable but the better companies can test with as little as $500–$1000. If they really believe in your project they will let you pay that $1000 out of your KS earnings after the campaign is over.

So, the funding company makes the ads and using Facebook apps, can selectively target people who have demonstrated that they buy things from Facebook that are similar to your product. Without getting into the costs to place ads in FB users' news feeds, I'll keep it simple by saying that their target is to get a minimum of a 3:1 ROAS (return on ad spend). This means for every $1 they spend, they get $3 back from sales on your site. If the ads convert at this ratio or higher they can then pump money into "buying lots of Facebook"–or lots of individual news feeds from their target market that Facebook helps them find for you. This is where the funding company is valuable–they have access to millions of dollars and will use as much as they can to get ROAS.

So what's in it for the funding company? Well, they don't come cheap, but for many project owners, they are invaluable in generating sales and income. On the low end a funding company will ask for 15% of the raised funds that they generated + the money they spend on the ads. On the high end they will ask for about 30%.

Confused? **Let's use an example:**

> *My Kickstarter is in full swing, and I reached my $10,000 goal on the first day. It's now day 4 and my campaign is at $20k. I give a funding company $1000 to run test ads with the agreement that if their ads don't test well, they don't go any further. The funding company spends my $1000 in a few days on multiple ads and determines that one ad in particular converts customers at a 4:1 ratio. The funding company then spends $25k of their own money to place that ad on Facebook– and you see an additional $100k of revenue in your campaign. Keep in mind that over the course of your campaign you generated an additional $30k of revenue on your own or through the platform itself (Kickstarter).*
>
> *So your revenue at the end looks like this: **$20k + $30k + $100k = $150k.** So how much do you have to pay the funding company out of your campaign? Well they are going to want their $25k back that they gave to Facebook + the $1000 you gave them and then 15% of that $100k they raised for you. So it should look like **$25k + $1k + $15k = $41k** add in that Kickstarter and other platforms take close to 10% of the total raise–so subtract out an additional $15K = $56K. **$150K – $56K = $94K.***
>
> *So you now have **$94k** after KS fees deposited in your bank account, whereas if you didn't use the funding company, you would have had $50k - KS fees of $5k = **$45k** deposited in your bank account.*

It's really not about coming up with that one idea that makes you big money. It's about coming up with a lot of ideas and letting the market decide what they like—i.e. **multiple failures to find the success.**

Now you might be thinking—ok, sure, they generated more sales but now I have to pay 3x the product because they boosted my sales three fold? This is where you have to know your margins. If you are charging 6x your product cost on your campaign your profit margin went down on the crowdfunded sales but you still made profit on each sale and that's why you chose to partner with them.

Why you should fail often and hard

Ok, here's the part you might not have been expecting or wanted to hear. Yes, you are going to have failures and *if you're successful, you're probably going to have lots of failures.* In fact, **I'm going to make a case why you should look forward to your failures.**

Most businesses fail. Most products fail. Most successful entrepreneurs have had many, many failures. So, if you're going to be a successful entrepreneur with your own signature brand—yep, you are going to have lots of failures. One could conclude that if you learn to embrace your failures instead of going into depression, you will be able to fail more often, fail faster and hopefully cheaper, and move on to the next experiment. It's really not about coming up with that one idea that makes you big money. It's about coming up with a lot of ideas and letting the market decide what they like—i.e. multiple failures to find the success.

You can read about the NIKE story in the book, "Shoe Dog"—the story of Phil Knight, Nike's founder. In the book, you learn how the company had numerous failures—even failures while experiencing other failures. You begin to wonder how NIKE ever became a multi-billion-dollar company and a household name.

Some failures can ruin a company, while others can be classified as setbacks. Some setbacks can definitely make you want to give up. However, it's the tenacious and humble artist who is able to pick himself up and ask, "Where did I go wrong? What should I have done? What would I do differently? What is my next move?"

> It's the tenacious and humble artist who is able to pick himself up and ask:
>
> **Where did I go wrong?**
>
> **What should I have done?**
>
> **What would I do differently?**
>
> **What is my next move?**

> **Beginning artists often hate failure so much it paralyzes them from taking risks that could lead to great successes.**

The plight of the artist/entrepreneur is often overwhelming optimism. Artists love what they do and are excited to do it, often creating denial when evaluating the merits or weaknesses of projects or products that they are working on. The seasoned entrepreneur learns to invest only as much time in a project as necessary to create a competent prototype or sample. Even though we don't want our projects to fail, it's much easier to recover if failure is fast and cheap.

Beginning artists often hate failure so much it paralyzes them from taking risks that could lead to great successes. Therefore, you should look forward to getting your inevitable failures out of the way so you can get on with the successes that are just around the corner. Usually you cannot accurately predict how your project is going to be received by your audience without making it and releasing it. You just have to use trial and error to guide you closer the successes you're bound to discover. Keep in mind that your failures shape you, sharpen you, and help you become successful—this is a very backwards but correct way of thinking, compared to what we were mostly taught in school. In school, your mistakes on papers and tests were met with lower grades, teaching us that mistakes are bad. They aren't.

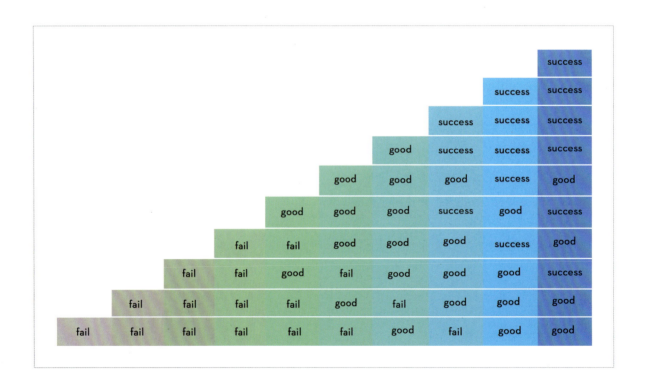

CREATING YOUR OWN BRAND

© Tim Lee, used with permission.

I'm more of a gallery artist– should I have a brand?

Yes, many artists who do not define themselves as illustrators create a brand with their work. Tim Lee used to create a lot of illustration work for clients but has transitioned into being more of a gallery artist. In fact, he is the co-founder of ODDCO, a gallery/bar in Pittsboro, NC that carries his work as well as work by a few other selected artists. Tim has branded his art on everything from prints to sculptures, jewelry, and apparel in his gallery *(shown above)*. Tim also sells his work through many other galleries.

Just because you want to create art and sell it for money doesn't mean you have to label yourself as a "gallery artist." You could own a gallery like Tim does, or never sell through a gallery. Many artists make a really nice living selling exclusively online. The key is to think of your art as an integrated product line featuring your style. This isn't something you can create overnight and it will take an extraordinary amount of work, but you can do it if you are committed.

I can't seem to get started on my dream project

I have received many, many emails asking me how to basically get started on a project. The person contacting me explains that they just can't seem to get started and that they don't know why. They state that they are excited about the project and that it's a dream project, yet they never seem to get going on it. Let me make a few suggestions on why this might be happening and how to combat it.

I believe that in most cases when artists have a dream project, but can't seem to get started on it, they are afraid that they won't be able to make art that is worthy of the vision they have in their head. Often, the solution is to do nothing, and by doing nothing, the artist can view their imaginary project in its perfect form…forever. Artists who regularly produce original work and original projects/products don't have this problem. They have an idea, do some research, complete preliminary sketches, take notes, schedule time, and then dive in systematically, making incremental advances towards the finished project.

If you have had a project that you've always wanted to complete, but can't seem to get started let me suggest the following:

1. ***Shelve the big project***—*you can always come back to it and it's not getting done anyway.*

2. ***Think of a much smaller project*** *and I mean really small. You need to teach yourself that you can start, execute, and finish a project. It could be as small as a three-painting or three-drawing series. It could be the face cards in a deck of cards. It could be a comic strip or a holiday gift card set. Whatever you choose, it must be small enough that you can start on it without procrastinating. If it's just completing a more complex image than you have started, then do that. The key here is that it must be something that you can start without putting too much thought into it.*

3. ***Now that you have completed a tiny project, pick a slightly larger project.*** *Then pick a larger one after that. You have to train your brain that you are capable of starting and completing a project. You need a number of wins in your creative bank account that tell you, "I did this; therefore, I can do that."*

   Without proving to yourself that you can start and finish over and over, negative self-talk will take over and your artistic paralysis will continue.

"There are many lessons you can learn at a (full- or part-time) job that will help you work for yourself, should you decide to transition to working as an independent artist."

GETTING A FULL-TIME ART JOB

There are many "in-house" artist jobs that can be found in many different types of businesses and agencies. I'm going to give some general advice that can be applied to all of them.

Working a full-time or part-time art job is going to require a few more skills than working from your home office or studio. Yes, you are competing with your own portfolio, but also with your appearance and your personality. All three are going to have to be attractive to an employer and, make no mistake, this is a competition. In many cases, the fourth factor often comes down to who you know. Not fair? I agree, but it's the world we live in.

Many freelance illustrators and gallery artists began working a full- or part-time art job for a company or institution. There are many lessons you can learn at a job that will help you work for yourself should you decide to transition to working as an independent artist.

Following is a partial list of art-related jobs:

- **Advertising Director**
- **Logo designer**
- **Graphic designer**
- **Packaging designer**
- **Typographer**

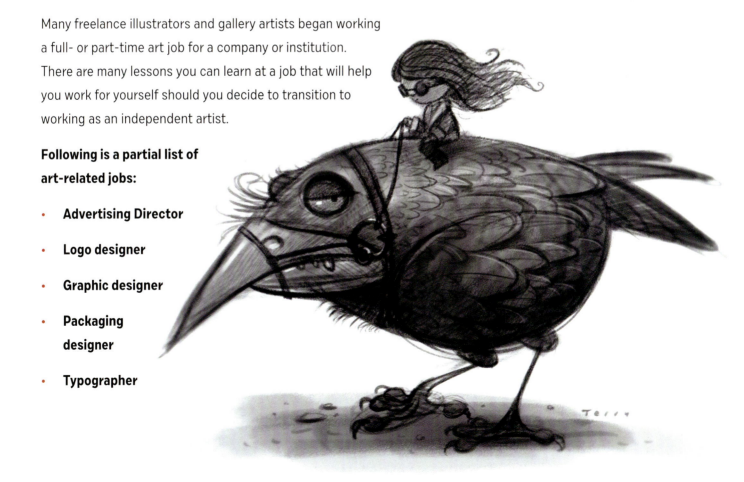

- **Architectural illustrator**
- **Publishing/editorial illustrator**
- **Children's Book illustrator**
- **Set and stage designer**
- **Playground/theme park designer**
- **Animator**
- **Concept artist**
- **Web designer**
- **Video game designer**

Finding jobs in your area can be challenging at times, but putting the word out that you are looking is a great way to start. From the many students I've taught over the years, most of them have obtained their art jobs from word-of-mouth. Yes, the classified ads in your area are going to list some of the jobs, but that is the first place that people look, so there will be lots of competition. Letting your friends, family, and social media contacts know what you are looking for will probably yield better results.

> **Tips to help you land that job you want**
> - *Save the most outlandish appearance...*
> - *Smile and be positive.*
> - *Establish a rapport with the interviewer.*
> - *Make sure you are well groomed.*
> - *Be on time!*
> - *Bring a sample of your work to leave behind.*
> - *Do your homework about the company you want to work for.*
> - *Sell your abilities but don't be cocky.*
> - *Non-verbal communication is very important*
> - *Don't appear desperate.*

Here are some tips to help you land that job you want:

1. You're creative and you like to express yourself with your appearance, but often the manager tasked with filling the position wants someone that fits in. **Save the most outlandish clothing, makeup, and accessories for your first day on the job…or wait even longer.**

2. Smile and be positive. Managers are afraid of negativity infiltrating the office. Negative people are a drain. If you're negative by nature, you'll have to figure out how to be positive or you'll have a hard time landing a job. **Try to find some personal anecdote to establish a rapport with the interviewer.** "Oh, is that you skiing (in the photo)? I used to ski back home in Colorado." Any personal connection will not only make you appear more human, it will also make you more memorable.

3. I shouldn't have to include this, but **make sure you are well groomed**. Teeth, hair, fingernails cut, clean clothes, etc.

GETTING A FULL TIME ART JOB

4. **Be on time!** Why would I hire you if you can't even show up on time to your interview?

5. **Bring a sample of your work to leave behind.** Once you walk out that door, your interview evaporates...unless you leave a color sample of your work with the interviewer. It just might be the thing that the hirer remembers and ultimately gets you hired simply because you've left something tangible.

6. **Do your homework and know about the company you want to work for.** It's flattering to a manager to realize that you've done your due diligence and know about the problems they face and the tasks you will be responsible for if you get the job.

7. **Sell your abilities but don't be cocky.** This isn't the time for false modesty, nor is it the time to overstate your skills. This is the time to let them know what you can do while leaving room for humility. "I know my way around Photoshop but there is still a lot to learn–it's a huge program."

> From the many students I've taught over the years, most of them have obtained their art jobs from word-of-mouth.

8. **Non-verbal communication is very important and could make or break your chances.** Nobody likes a weak, limp, fishy, handshake so make it firm! Don't turn it into a contest, but put something behind that handshake that says, "I'm here and I'm excited." Also, good eye contact is a must. If you're shy and hate to look people in the eyes, the interviewer sees this a sign of weakness and ineffectiveness.

9. **Don't appear desperate to get the job.** There are other opportunities out there and saying something like, "I really need this job," or "I hope I get this so I can pay my bills" are turn offs. I know, it's the truth, but some truths need not be spoken at certain times. The employer knows you need money or you wouldn't be applying, but human nature is that we want our employees to be leading happy, healthy, stress-free lives...before they hire you.

118 WILL TERRY *What They Don't Teach in Art School*

Job security

You've heard all the common things you need to do to keep your job secure, but let me throw out a few more that you might not have thought of.

First, you need to become indispensable. Seth Godin popularized this idea in his book "Linchpin" in which he explains that in order to be the first one hired and the last one fired, you need to provide more value than the average employee. Volunteer to help on tasks when volunteers are requested. Ask if you can learn how to do more jobs, tasks, or assignments that are not in your everyday work. You can also make suggestions to improve the business, and if your ideas are used, you will be looked at as providing more value than most of your co-workers. If you are the employee that managers rely on because you work harder, know more about the business, and know how to do more tasks, you will be indispensable.

Second, try to become a manager. Managers typically have more job security than individual workers. Artists that work for institutions or businesses have the inherent problem that their managers are often not creating art. So, if you become a manager overseeing one or two artists at a company, you likely won't make art. If making art is all you want to do, then becoming a manager in this scenario doesn't make much sense. However, in publishing companies or businesses that have an art department, there are management jobs where you still get to have your hands *on* the art.

Graphic designers often take "art director" positions, but the two titles are very similar. Art directors decide which illustrators to hire, what typefaces, colors, textures, and graphic elements to use. Art directors and graphic designers often answer to the title, "Creative Director." Creative directors are managers over art directors, graphic designers, photographers, and sometimes editors. So, how do you get a job as a creative director? This is where it requires you to get a little creative—no pun intended.

Many creative directors are hired as the only artist, graphic designer, or art director at their company. For example, an artist might ask her employer if her job can be retitled to "Creative Director." That's it. Then when the artist applies for a creative director position at another company, she can say she has previous experience as a creative director.

A few tips for keeping your job secure:
- *First, you need to become indispensable.*
- *Second, try to become a manager.*
- *Third, do all of the things you should have learned when you were a kid.*

Third, do all of the things you should have learned when you were a kid. Be on time, be friendly and easy to work with, don't leave early, always tell the truth—even if it makes you look bad, and make sure your attitude reflects your desire and willingness to help the company succeed. Just doing these things alone will help ensure that the company lets someone else go before you.

How much money can I expect to earn?

This is perhaps the most interesting topic to art students and it almost never gets discussed in art school. While it's going to be hard to lay out exact numbers, the general message I want to convey is that an employer is never going to pay you as much as you want or feel you deserve. Freelancers, while running the risk of going without enough assignment work, also benefit from being able to set their own prices and can take as much work as they can handle. Most successful freelance artists earn more than those who work in-house.

I know artists who are working small art jobs for minimum wage all the way up to a few hundred thousand dollars per year. In many parts of the U.S., the standard entry-level graphic design job will usually pay between $35,000 and $55,000 per year. Graphic designers can work their way up to $60-$80k in many parts of the U.S., while senior designers in major cities can often break into the six-figure range. Understand that many of these jobs also come with benefits such as medical and retirement. And smaller companies often offer stock options.

GETTING A FULL TIME ART JOB

"When you help your client solve problems, you become that person they want to work with again and again. You become a team member."

PROFESSIONAL PRACTICES

Pricing your work

You need to learn how to price your work to maximize your profits and compete with other artists. Nobody likes the feeling that they are leaving money on the table or that they lost the job because they asked for way too much money. I'll help you figure out how to think when you assess the value of your work and how to ask clients to pay you what you want.

Let's start with the idea that there is no such thing as a "going rate." Almost every beginning illustrator wants to know what the going rate is so they can feel comfortable quoting it to their client and getting paid what everyone else is getting paid. Unfortunately, there is no such rate. Why? Because you are creating art—not working on an assembly line factory floor assembling the same part all day, every day.

Each piece of art you create takes a different amount of time with different parameters and different challenges with different sizes and levels of complexity in both content and concept. Hypothetically, if you gave the same assignment

to ten different illustrators, each would create a different solution that took a different amount of time to complete. On top of that, each artist has a different workload with different financial obligations and different levels of ambition. *One price does not–and should not–fit all.*

If I asked you to hand-dig a large hole in my backyard so I could install a Koi pond, and I said, "The going rate is $2/hour," would you want to work for that price? I wouldn't either. Let's say you want the fish pond in your backyard, and the going rate is $20/hour, but the kid asking to dig it is only ten years old? A twenty-year-old, fit person could probably dig twice as fast as the ten-year-old kid, so it will cost about twice as much if you hire the kid at the going rate of $20/hour.

A going rate doesn't work unless the workers are all capable of the same output and the job is about the same. Illustration work and illustrators have too many variables to set standard pricing–some have tried, but it never works.

If you weren't already convinced that looking for or charging the "going rate" isn't a smart way to price your work, let me try one more time to convince you. I want you to imagine yourself in three different futures or alternate universes.

1) You are offered $1000 to make an illustration and the subject matter is going to be fun to work on. You haven't had work in a long time and you're struggling to make your rent or mortgage payment this month. $1000 would help you send off your rent and pay a few other bills.

2) Same $1000 job–everything is the same except you also have $5000 in your bank account, and you have a few other illustration jobs paying about the same.

3) Same $1000 job–same scenario, but you are swamped with illustration work. You are working 7 days/week and will invoice $15,000 this month to various clients.

So the question is–do you feel the same about the job in each scenario? Would your desire to take the assignment fluctuate in each scenario? Would you feel like asking the client for more money if you are in situation #3? I would. I would–and have–tripled or quadrupled the amount I would have asked for if I was in situation #1–many times. Why would I ever care what someone else would charge?

> **There is no such thing as a "going rate."** Each piece of art you create takes a different amount of time with different parameters and different challenges with different sizes and levels of complexity in both content and concept.

> A going rate doesn't work unless the workers are all capable of the same output and the job is about the same. Illustration work and illustrators have too many variables to set standard pricing–some have tried, but it never works.

PROFESSIONAL PRACTICES

My situation was, has been, and will be different from other artists, and even different in my own life… my situation will always fluctuate. If I have to virtually kill myself working overtime, on holidays, weekends, late at night, etc. to take on more work, why would I worry about charging "the going rate"? I'll charge what I want—sometimes it will be low when I really need the work and fear losing the job if I charge too much. Sometimes I'll charge a really high fee, risking losing the job because my plate is already full and taking on more work would be a huge inconvenience.

"But how do I know how much to charge? I have to quote my client a price and I have no idea where to start? I don't know if my client is thinking $500 or $5000." Right! This is the problem we are going to tackle, but first we need to establish and understand another simple concept—that is, that the value of goods and services are always fluctuating. For example, let's look at the price of a bottle of water. You can pick up a case of thirty-six bottles of water at a box store for $3–$4–that's about ten cents per bottle! At a gas station, the same bottle of water could cost $1.29, and at an amusement park, it could cost $5 or more. There are times where you wouldn't think of buying a bottle of water at a gas station because you aren't thirsty and you can get a free drink of water where you are going in a few minutes. On the other hand, if your car broke down and you've been stuck in one-hundred-degree temperatures for a few hours, you probably wouldn't hesitate to pay for an overpriced "convenient" cold bottle of

PROFESSIONAL PRACTICES

water at a gas station. So, the value fluctuates based on your situation at the time.

You have various reasons for wanting to take on an illustration assignment and each one will fluctuate at different times during your career. Illustrators usually take freelance assignments based on the amount of money they will be paid, but there are other factors for taking a job. Perhaps you are asked to work with a company you've always loved and working with them would feel prestigious to you. Maybe you sail boats as a hobby and you are asked to illustrate a children's book about sailing? Many illustrators would be willing to work for a lower fee if they love the subject matter they've been asked to work on. Or maybe your favorite aunt asks you to illustrate her book, and you feel an obligation to help. Or you are starting out and you don't have any printed work in your portfolio, but are willing to work on subject matter you're not that fond of just to get the portfolio pieces. All of these reasons can factor into the amount of money you are willing to settle for.

The value of goods and services is always fluctuating.

Ok, back to your client...they have asked how much you will charge to illustrate their children's book.

First order of business: fact finding. You need to find out as much about the project as possible. What is their deadline and how many pages will you need to illustrate? How many individual illustrations will you need to create, including the cover? How complex is each illustration? Are there multiple figures? Crowd scenes? Will you have to generate the concepts for each illustration, or do they supply the ideas? It's more work if you have to concept the book. How many copies will be printed and distributed? Is your client giving away the printed work as a service or promotion, or are they charging the customer? The "usage" for your work is usually factored into the client's budget and you need to know how it's being used to charge more or less.

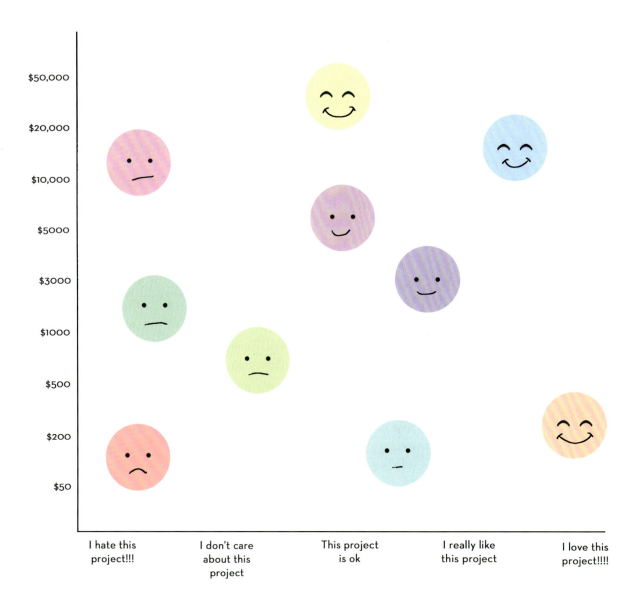

128 WILL TERRY *What They Don't Teach in Art School*

> **You need to know where your bottom line is before you enter into negotiations. Your bottom line is the price where, if the client offers one dollar less, your immediate answer is "No."** *(AND you feel really good about saying it.)*

Next, calculate how much time you estimate to complete the project. This isn't easy because there will be alterations requested from the client and, without having worked for them in the past, you don't know how easy or difficult it will be. Then figure out how much money you'll need for the entire project. Most clients won't work with you on an hourly rate because they don't know how slow or fast you are, so they will most likely prefer a flat fee. The amount of money you will need is going to vary depending on your financial situation, how much time you have, if you have other work, etc. Let's say you think, based on the conversation you had with your client, that the project—including sketches, revisions, and final art—will take you about 300 hours total. At $10/hour, you would get about $3,000 and at $20/hour – $6,000 and so on. Keep in mind that if you work faster than you thought and if the client is easy to work with, you could earn a much higher hourly rate.

Okay, so now you've decided that you will need $6,000 to complete this project. **Is that your bottom line?** What if you ask for $6k and they counter with $4k, stating that's all they have in their budget? Now we need to talk about your "bottom line," or the lowest amount of money you will accept. You really want to do this job, but $4000 is much lower than you want. You have to decide if the subject matter, the printed work, and the amount of work is still worth it at $4k. If yes, then I would ask you… what if they offered you $3k? You need to know where your bottom line is before you enter into negotiations. *Your bottom line is the price where, if the client offers one dollar less, your immediate answer is "No." (AND you feel really good about saying it.)*

So let's say that your bottom line is $3,500, but you asked for $6,000 and the client offered you $4,000. Your answer should be yes, even though you aren't super excited about the price—at least it was higher than your bottom line. But what if your bottom line was $5k, you asked for $6k, and they offered $4k? You should be happy to tell them no, but let them know that you would be willing to work for $5k or you might be willing to work for $4k if they were willing to reduce the number of illustrations, reduce the complexity of the drawings, or give you more autonomy on the direction of the art. Sometimes clients will give up control if you will agree to a low price…but you'll have to ask for it.

But what if you asked for $6k, your bottom line was $5k and they say yes to $6k? Now you're wondering how much money they would have been willing to pay? $10k? $15k? More? This is a problem, but one that often cannot be solved when negotiating contracts. However, following are a few suggestions on how to reduce the amount of money you're "leaving on the table."

1. Creatively exaggerate your situation and say something like: "I'm really excited about the possibility of working on this book—I can fall in love with it and deliver my best work! I'm really busy right now and would need to be able to fit it into my schedule. Can you tell me what your budget is? I'm hoping I'll be able to work within it" (it being the potential client's budget).

   By using wording like this you place your client in the awkward position of defending his entire budget. Whereas they might have wanted you to throw out the first number, you have now put them in the position of proving to you that they have enough money to hire you. Often when they do give you their budget, it's much higher than your ask was going to be; but you're going to have to be confident in your voice or written word.

2. If the client won't divulge his budget and again requests that you provide your bid, you can try to determine what artists working on similar projects were paid. This information is often impossible to find unless you have friends or acquaintances who have worked for the same company or similar companies. Asking other illustrators to give you a price range is a good start but you're still shooting in the dark. At this point, I would do this: You want $6k, your bottom line is $5k, so I would ask for $7-8k. If they only have $5k, it's not that far from $7k so your price doesn't look meaningless if you accept $5k. If they agree to $8k you just got an extra $2k over what you felt you needed! Yes, there might be money left on the table, but what you are getting besides the work and money is the experience; and over time you'll be able to command higher prices and max out the budgets of your clients.

Should I ask for more money?

This question assumes that your client made you a money offer along with the assignment, so they threw out the first number. When you first start out, all of this will feel really weird and you are probably not going to feel comfortable asking for more money. You need to know that it's very common for illustrators to ask for the offer to be bumped up a little bit. How much? Usually 10-30% is what's normal for many illustrators to request.
Example: Your client offers you $1000 for a full-page illustration and you ask if they can bump it to $1,200.

PROFESSIONAL PRACTICES

By asking for more money, you put yourself in the "normal" category of illustrators asking for more money. You don't need to worry that the request will make the client back out and hire another illustrator. It's not their money and if they have it in their budget, they will often give it to you; if they don't, they simply cannot.

Often, art buyers have wiggle room in their budgets to offer you a little extra money and, as a freelancer, if you make it a habit to ask, it can result in thousands of extra dollars each year. Usually, a client won't have that much extra to work with if they initially gave you their budget. Company creative departments set budgets for their art directors to offer illustrators and they often give them discretionary money in the 10-20% range. This means that if they offer you $5k, they might be able to go up $5,500 or $6,000—but don't ask them to double their budget, because they probably just can't go that high.

> **Often, art buyers have wiggle room in their budgets to offer you a little extra money and, as a freelancer, if you make it a habit to ask, it can result in thousands of extra dollars each year.**

Contracts

Now we're getting into the subjects that most artists dread, including me. When I started out, I hated even *thinking* about the paperwork, but if you want to realize your dream as a professional artist, you're going to have to face it head on.

Most companies that you will work for will insist that you sign their contract before you can begin working for them. Sometimes, however, you will be asked to begin work as they are still preparing your contract. In this case, you will have to decide if you want to work before you have a signed contract. I must point out, however, that if you aren't willing to get going right away, you can lose a job based on the insanely quick deadlines that often follow projects like these. If you tell your art director that you want to wait for the contract, they might cancel with you and go with another more willing illustrator.

Ok, so now you have the contract and you want to know if it's a standard deal that most other artists receive, or are they sneaking horrible, overreaching terms into it? This is a great time to have made friends or acquaintances with working illustrators so you can compare your contract to some of theirs.

PROFESSIONAL PRACTICES

In general, most contracts have fairly standard asks and demands that often sound harsh, but when broken down are usually reasonable requests.

As I am not a licensed attorney, I cannot give you contract advice. I would suggest that you find a friend who is good at breaking down and comprehending "legalese." Or find another illustrator–one who has a good track record working with the kind of clients you're looking for–to help you.

Should I sign a "Work for Hire" contract?

You will often hear other illustrators scream, "NEVER SIGN A WORK FOR HIRE!!!" Then they will bang on about how predatory and evil the company is, who sends artists these kinds of contracts. I prefer a more nuanced answer to arm the artist with a better understanding of when and when *not* to enter into a WFH contract.

A WFH contract basically states that you, the contractor or artist, are signing away any and all rights to the work you are about to create. Many of these contracts state that the artist cannot claim the work when it is completed, and that the artist cannot display the work in his portfolio or use the work to promote himself in any way. Most often, when you sign a WFH contract, you agree to a flat fee for the work–no royalties and no other benefits from the work. If the client wishes, they can sell the artist's work to another company at a profit without compensating you. If the client starts another project with your work again, you get nothing. Legally the client becomes the creator of the artist's work.

So, what does the artist get? Money and experience and that's about it. Sometimes, the contract does not specify that you cannot use the art in your portfolio, so you *can* use artwork created through

agreements such as this to gain more client work. I would push back on this part of the contract with my client and ask them directly, "Do you mind if we cross out this part because I really want to use this art in my portfolio?" In many cases, the client got the contract from an attorney who copied this part of the contract because every other WFH contract contains the portfolio clause. Often your client won't care about that part of the contract and will amend it in your favor, but you have to ask.

You have to weigh the pros and cons in every contract you enter into and my advice is not to let peer pressure from other artists influence your decisions. The artists who brag about never signing WFH contracts are often out of work and who knows if they are being completely honest? They aren't paying your bills—you are, and you need to evaluate each opportunity on your own terms. I have turned down a lot of WFH contracts, but I've also taken my fair share.

PROFESSIONAL PRACTICES

Copyright

I want to give you some general advice regarding copyright law and your work. You can learn all of the legal aspects of copyright law on your country's website. I cannot possibly give specific advice that pertains to everyone's situation, but here are some general things to think about and of course my perspective is based in United States copyright law.

I have been a freelance illustrator for twenty-seven years and out of the thousands of illustration jobs I have done, I've never had a company steal my work. In addition, I've only known of a few cases among all of my illustration friends around the world in which they have had work stolen; and out of those few cases, I've NEVER known an artist to have successfully taken a company to court and won a judgment. Keep in mind that even if I did know of an artist winning a judgment, that's only half the battle. You would then have to collect your money, and companies have all kinds of ways of stalling, filing for bankruptcy, or just deciding not to pay. Do you have enough money to retain an attorney to continue to bring that delinquent client back before a judge?

> In general, companies don't make it a regular practice to steal work from artists—they just don't want to be smeared on social media, and many company owners and managers are honest. They realize that theft doesn't make a good part of a business plan, so infractions are extremely rare.

My point is that, in general—small, mid-sized, and large companies don't make it a regular practice to steal work from artists—they just don't want to be smeared on social media and many company owners and managers are honest. They realize that theft doesn't make a good part of a business plan, so infractions are extremely rare.

Keep in mind that I have had lots of my fanart stolen and used on products produced in Asia and marketed online. I have chosen to keep my sanity intact by ignoring these infractions. Why not go after them? If you actually look into the amount of time and money it would take to successfully prosecute or even file complaints, take down notices, etc., you would find how exhausting and time-consuming it is. I choose to continue to create art instead of "playing lawyer". It's a personal choice and I understand why some artists work really hard to try to stop the theft of their work; but in the end, I think it costs you more in time, money, and stress—it's part of the business.

If you live in the U.S., you have the option of registering your copyrights on each work you create at the U.S. copyright office. You can also wait until you have ten, twenty, or fifty pieces in order to save money on filing fees. Why register your copyrights? It allows you to sue for triple damages if you take a thief to court. You would have to prove how much money you lost based on the theft, and then the court could award you damages times three. Again, I don't personally know any artists who bother to register their copyrights. Often publishers register the copyrights to the books they publish each year and that protects you should another party decide to steal the work produced for the book.

You need to also understand that in the U.S., your copyright is inherent when you create the artwork. In other words, you own your copyright after you create a piece of art—it's not a race between you and a thief to get to the copyright office and file. If someone was to fraudulently register a copyright for a work you created, it would probably be fairly easy to prove you are the creator based on your body of work, digital file origination dates, preliminary work on the art in question, etc.

I have created over 4,000 pieces of art in my career as an illustrator, and not once have I found an infraction from a company here in the U.S. But let's say that for the past twenty-seven years, every six months I gathered up my work, scanned it, cataloged each piece, entered each piece in a database, filled out the online application for each piece—twenty-seven years times two (every six months) = fifty-four submissions. 4,000 pieces of art ÷ fifty-four = seventy-four pieces of art and forms to fill out, and roughly fifty-five dollars to submit every six months, which equals $2,970. But for me, it's not the money as much as the amount of time it would take to fill out the forms and keep track of each piece of art.

In the end, you have to decide if this is something that is important to you. I'm sure there are a few anecdotal stories where an artist won a big judgment against a company, but I haven't heard of one. I'm not giving you legal advice—just sharing my thoughts on when and when *not* to copyright your work.

Invoicing

Yes, you're going to have to deal with words like "invoice"—yuck. You didn't become artists to have to do the dirty work, but this is an easy one and once you get set up, it's a breeze. An invoice is just a bill you send your client so you can get paid; and getting paid is fun, so let's dive in!

You can create an invoice in a Google doc or some other word processor and I'm sure there are many other options out there. A standard invoice from an artist is formatted to fit a vertical 8.5" x 11" piece of paper. Most artists send theirs digitally now, so size probably doesn't matter; however, some clients print them out for their files, so keeping a standard size will be easier for them.

An invoice has some of your personal information that the client will need in order to pay you in compliance with Federal and local tax laws. It also contains other information specific to the job you are billing them for, and it needs to have some of their information on it. Sometimes you will work multiple times for the same client, so keeping accurate invoices will help both of you determine which job you are getting paid for, or which payment you are missing.

Here is an example of an invoice—this is actually my invoice from my Google doc. You will notice that I put a little illustration at the top. I like to warm up my business documents a little bit, as another reminder to the art director that I love what I do.

Next, I add the **date** that I send out the invoice. Some artists also put the date they began working on the project.

Invoice

Date: 6/12/2021

Job invoice number: 033065

Contract #

Due Date:

Commissioned by: Jane Doe

Client: The Best Client Ever

Amount: $15,000.00

Description: 5 digital paintings of penguins playing and having a party

Total: $15,000

Will Terry
61 north 705 west
Orem Ut 84057

PROFESSIONAL PRACTICES

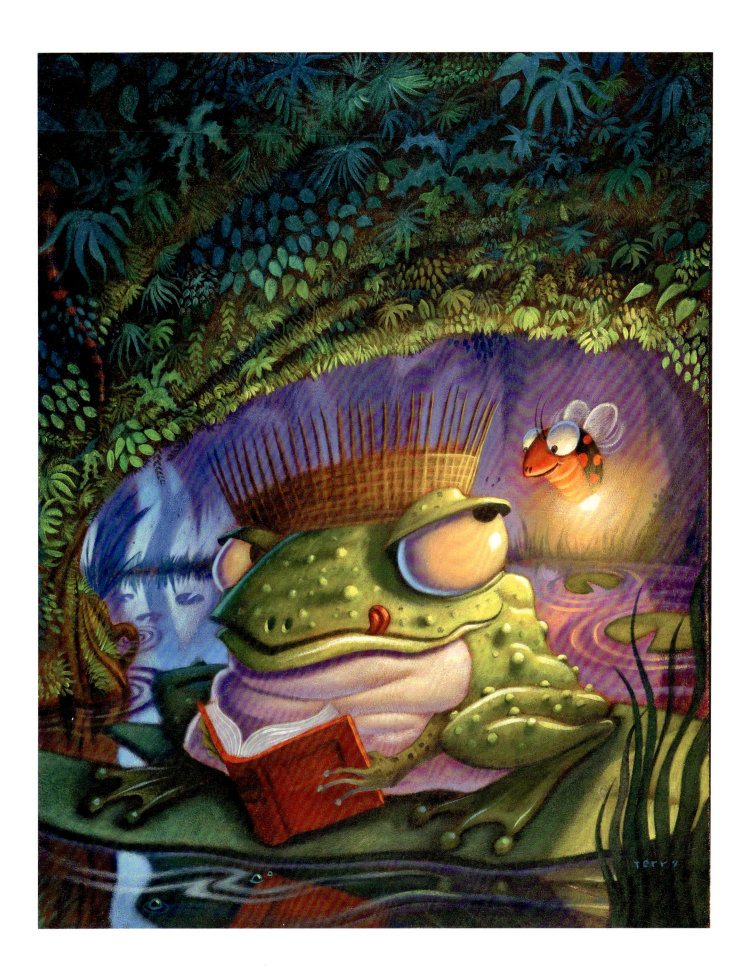

Then I include a **job number**—this is my own number, and each time I create an invoice, the number is increased by one. You can come up with any numbering system that works for you. I suggest NOT starting with 0001 since there aren't many clients that want to know they are your first. You can start anywhere because it's your job number—start with 0023 or 00740 or whatever you want.

Next, I have the **contract #** or you can use the **purchase order** or **P.O. #**. This is a number that the client will supply on the contract. It's good to put that on your invoice as it definitively links your invoice to your contract and is easier to track if something goes wrong. I also add the **due date**, which is the date that the artwork was due or the deadline. I put this on my invoice so that the billing department knows

that the clock (on paying me) should have started ticking the day I turned in the art. Sometimes you cannot invoice right away if you do not have all of the information for the invoice—thus the different dates.

Then I add "**Commissioned by**"—this is the name of the person who hired you. In most cases, it will be the art director, but it could also be the creative director, editor, or an art buyer. If the accounts payable department has a question, they can look to see who your contact was when they get your invoice. Then I put the name of the client on the invoice. In many cases, you will work for a publication that is owned by a parent company. It's important to ask your contact who they want listed as the client on your invoice.

Then I include the **amount I am owed**. There is space under the amount for me to add another field if I had to purchase supplies for the project that go beyond the normal scope of an illustration assignment. For instance, if I am painting a mural, I will bill for painting supplies because the costs will be substantial vs. working digitally. I cannot bill for my computer and tablet.

The **description** is next—this is a very important, as time will erode the best of memories and often you will forget what you actually *did* for a particular client. The description will jog your memory and the memory of your clients should you need to dig back into your history. Be specific, especially if there were multiple illustrations in the project.

The total should reflect the **sum of charges** and, in my case, it's usually just repeating the amount. If you have any questions about the amount you are charging your client, it's best to work that out via email or phone before you charge them for an amount they might dispute. Good communication will always save frustration and embarrassment.

Then you need to include your **personal identification information** so they can fill out their tax documentation accurately and send the payment to you.

Last, I include a **brief usage agreement** as a reminder for what they purchased. I want to have this in writing in case I see a usage violation. *Example: I sold them one-time North American reproductive rights and a friend shows me my illustration published in Japan.* In this case, I would have a dispute with my client and can choose how to proceed to attempt to collect any monies I feel I'm owed for the breach of contract by my client. These terms can be changed for each assignment you work on as well.

> **You don't want to be too aggressive or too passive following up on your payments.**

I send the invoice to my client after I deliver the artwork and the artwork has been accepted. I don't feel good sending them the invoice when I'm still making alterations to the artwork. Most companies are on a thirty-to sixty-day-billing cycle. Meaning that they will usually pay you the next month or the month after. You don't want to be too aggressive or too passive following up on your payments. Collecting is one of the worst parts of this business, but the good news is that most clients pay on their schedule… you just might have to wait longer for your money than you want to.

I think it's fine to gently poke your client towards the end of the thirty-day cycle just to let them know that you are there. Keep in mind that your art director or editor isn't responsible for paying you—the accounts payable department is. If you take out your frustrations on your art director, you might never get asked to work for them again. I send an email to my art director like this:

Hi John,

Hope all is well with you and your family.

I really had fun working on our last project, the dragon dancing. I really hope we can work together again soon!

Anyway, I just wanted to ask you for your contact in accounts payable to see if they are close to sending out my check? Do you have a name and email address I can use to check on that?

Thank you,

Will

This puts little-to-no pressure on your art director, while letting him or her know that you have no animosity towards them—you just want to hunt down your money and leave them alone. I've known illustrators to get really upset with their art director over a payment, expecting to be hired again. If I were an art director, I'd probably choose to work with easy-to-get-along-with artists.

Working with art directors

It's important to understand who you're going to be working with and what makes them tick. Many art directors have aspirations of doing exactly what you're doing—freelance illustration. They got the art director job, hoping to one day transition into creating the artwork. In fact, some of your art directors are probably working towards this goal after work. They love art and love being part of the creative process just like you do. Often, they don't get credit in the publication for making your work look great.

PROFESSIONAL PRACTICES

Art directors have to protect themselves against underperforming illustrators and that's why it can be really hard for you to get hired for your first gigs. If you haven't illustrated any freelance assignments, you are unproven and, therefore, *scary* for an art director to take a chance on. You need to work hard to create a portfolio that doesn't look like you just stepped out of art school, even though you might have. You need work that looks like it was completed for an actual paid project. This is where working for free can actually come in handy—you should consider offering your services in exchange for printed material.

Ok, so when you have your first job, you don't want to mess things up. Here's some advice on **maintaining your relationship**:

1. Have fun in your back-and-forth emails, and don't be afraid to write things like, "I can't wait to get started!" or "This is going to be a blast!" or "I'm going to have fun designing these characters." **Let your contact know that you are excited because he or she wants to get your best work**, and he knows that unless you're excited, you can't give him your best.

2. Before you talk to the art director on the phone, go through any material pertaining to the job, thinking about how you will start. **Then take notes and ask questions to clarify anything you're unsure about.** Never "wing it" hoping to read their minds to satisfy their desires. This will only give you more work when the art director asks you to make changes and it will make you look more amateurish.

143

3. **If your client can't explain what they want you to draw, this is a red flag.** Instead of drawing anyway, hoping to please them, you have to get them to understand that you cannot draw what you cannot visualize. *For example: If your client asks you to make a scene, both dark and bright at the same time (this happened to me), you are going to have a hard time pulling this off without lots of direction.* In my case, they wanted the piece to have a light airy watercolor feel, but they also wanted to show that it was pitch black at night with no moon or stars.

4. **Never lie to your client.** Even if you made a mistake in writing down the deadline or if you blew a sketch deadline or if you omitted a change, never lie or make up an excuse. If you want to be a pro, you have to act like a pro, and pros take responsibility even if the potential consequences are bad. In the end, you'll have your integrity and nobody but you can take that away. You're playing the long game.

5. **Compliment your art director on his contributions to the project.** If he sends you a layout with type treatments, chances are he took pride in that work. Endear your way into the hearts of your art directors with a few compliments—they go a long way.

6. **Be willing to make the alterations you will no doubt be asked to make.** Your client is paying you and they get to dictate the content of the art. The better clients will be light-handed, while the small clients with less experience will be heavy-handed and often hard to work with. If you're starting out, your goal is to work up to the big clients that will respect you for your contributions. Tough it out in the early years to build a better and more fulfilling career down the road.

7. **Under promise and over deliver.** If your client asks to have sketches by Friday, they would really appreciate you getting them to them on Friday morning or in the last few hours on Thursday. Sure, they said Friday, but they didn't mean end-of-day Friday because they want to look at the sketches and perhaps show others in the office to prepare for that Monday morning meeting with the whole team. Tell them you'll have them for Friday, but send them on Thursday—no earlier, or it will look like you didn't spend enough time on their project...and they might think you have more time for nit-picky changes.

8. **After the job is finished, send them an email explaining how much you liked working with them and how much you'd like to work for them in the future.** If other illustrators are doing this and you're not, you might be perceived as indifferent.

You are always busy

You are always busy. Even when you aren't busy, you ARE busy when communicating with clients or potential clients. It's okay to get a little creative in order to persuade clients to give us what we want. When a client asks you to work on an assignment, they don't say, "...and by the way, our third quarter was the lowest in the history of our company and we're expecting a lot of layoffs soon." In other words, they don't give you information that they don't think you need to know or that makes them look bad.

PROFESSIONAL PRACTICES

145

Likewise, you don't need to give information that doesn't make you look good. Making yourself look like your services are in demand is what I call "the yard sale principle."

> **The Yard Sale Principle**
>
> *Have you ever been to a yard sale and picked up an item that you thought, "Hmmm, this is really cool…I should buy this…I might buy this…"? Then you set it down and see someone else pick it up. Immediately, the value of the item goes up in your mind because the other person validated your positive opinion of the item by picking it up. Now you're wondering if they'll set it back down so you can get it or if they'll buy it, leaving you disappointed.*

When you say you are really busy with work, a potential client will think that you have a higher value because other clients are also picking you. *Never* say, "My schedule is wide open!" You might as well say, "Nobody wants or trusts me to work on their project but I'm hoping you will."

Giving your best, no matter how much money you are being paid

This was a hard concept for me to understand when I started freelancing in 1992. Logically, I thought that if a client offered me $300 for a narrative illustration, I should spend a lot less time than if they were offering me $3,000 for about the same amount of work. What I didn't realize is that different clients and different projects often come with vastly different budgets—it's just the nature of the business. In my mind, I thought the client should get what they paid for, but it was a big mistake and it cost me many clients in the beginning.

The client with the $300 budget saw the work in my portfolio—the work I spent a lot of time on to attract both the $300 *and* $3,000 clients. The $300 client doesn't know about the $3,000 client. The $300 client runs their business and tries to get the best work they can afford.

So, when I didn't give the $300 client my best work, they were let down and never hired me again. I did this quite often in the first few years.

As an artist, you must take pride in your work and look at your portfolio as your most prized possession. In fact, you shouldn't even allow your clients to define the value of your work. What I mean is that your criteria for quality should have nothing to do with the standards of your clients. Your standards should be higher than your clients'. I've adopted the mindset that while it's true that my clients pay for me to create art, it's my art and they GET to use it. However, I make it for me and it must pass *my* standards—regardless of whether it is good enough for the client—hours before I really start to polish it.

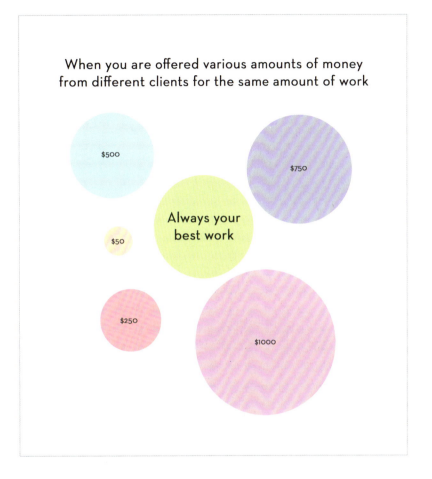

Be personable

There are two sides of the communication that you will have with your clients—the nuts and bolts details of the job, and the small talk human interaction stuff. Many beginners and a fair number of pros go into robot mode, making the mistake of only discussing the business side of their projects in a cold logical manner.

What makes you memorable to someone is the way you made them feel when you were with them. You can NOT afford to be forgettable. This business is hard enough without making it harder by skipping out on a fairly easy thing that will help you stand out. Look for opportunities to relate to your contacts beyond talking about illustration or the job. "I noticed your office is in Dallas—we had really good barbecue the last time we were through there." Anything you can do to toss in a little relatable anecdote can be the thing that kicks off a business relationship that lasts for years.

Be solution-oriented

Sometimes you will be faced with requests for illustration alterations from your art director that don't make sense. To clarify, you may get a request from your client that isn't a good fit or solution for your project. Sometimes it won't work because it conflicts with a part of the story, or it will ruin the composition or concept. In this case, you have a great opportunity to become part of the team instead of just the illustrator.

You could just tell your art director, "It won't work because of these reasons…" and then expect them to get back to you with a different solution. This is what most illustrators would do, but because you want to build your career and become indispensable to your clients, you need to use your intellect to help them. What a top shelf pro would do is understand *why* the client wants the changes they want, and then figure out a way to save the composition or story while accomplishing the goal that the art team was originally trying to solve. When you pitch your idea back to them, they might not like it, or they might love it; either way, their impression of you just went up a few clicks!

> What a top shelf pro would do is understand why the client wants the changes they want, and then figure out a way to save the composition or story while accomplishing the goal that the art team was originally trying to solve.

When you help your client solve problems, you become that person they want to work with again and again. You become a team member.

Time management

One of the hardest things you'll have to learn is how to predict how much time you will need for each assignment. In addition, you will have to learn how to work at different times during your days. This is because you won't always be able to work when you want because your clients might not give you approval to begin working when you want. You will often have to shift your attention to other projects or tasks that you weren't planning to do on a particular day.

You won't have a boss breathing down your neck monitoring your time spent on work or social media or video game distractions, etc. This can be a blessing or a curse, depending on your ability to plan your day and focus during the time periods you've set for specific work. Don't worry if you're not good at this now—most of us aren't built to be good at this stuff, but you can get good at it over time.

I suggest you keep a calendar for starters because if you know what's coming up, you will be less likely to forget about tasks that need to be done by specific dates. Next, I suggest freelancers plan out their weeks and days zooming in to the details of each hour. This isn't fun but neither is blowing a deadline or pulling an "emergency" all-nighter that didn't have to happen. If you schedule your time, you can plan for play time as well and it will be that much more enjoyable, knowing that it fits into your schedule rather than wrecks it.

One of my biggest strategies for time management is very simple—I plan to get all of my work done a week before it's due, if possible. There's always a friend or family member who will ask if you want to skip out on work to help them with something fun. There's always a car that needs to go into the shop, a sick spouse, you getting sick, a home repair, a dental appointment you forgot about, or shopping that needs to be done. Those who plan to use all the time they are given up to the last hour pull all-nighters and usually turn in substandard work.

All-nighters? Nope. They never worked for me because I was always busy enough that they just robbed the next day, catching up on sleep at two in the afternoon.

You can't get something for nothing and all-nighters demand repayment in full at some point. Without exception, my students who regularly pulled all-nighters were the bottom half of the artists in my classes. There's a direct correlation between artists who are poor planners and the quality of work they produce.

Managing money as an illustrator

I haven't met a single freelance illustrator who didn't struggle with managing their money in the early days of their career. Most of us have had multiple full and/or part time jobs before, during, and after college. Most of those jobs paid twice or once a month regularly and we got used to those regular paychecks. Sure, the amounts fluctuated up and down, based on how many hours we put in; but like clockwork, there was always a check on schedule.

PROFESSIONAL PRACTICES

Throw all of that out when starting your own freelance illustration business. You will either learn how to manage your money or suffer some pretty tough hardships as you'll learn by natural consequences. I guarantee that learning from my advice is more fun and will lower your stress level.

You will not always be able to control how many jobs you get, when they start, or when you finish them. But most importantly, you won't be able to control when you get your check. So, who would be crazy enough to work under these conditions? Well, you can actually make more money as a freelancer than working a similar in-house illustration job for starters. You can also choose when you want to work on your assignments and you can choose who NOT to work for—that's big. You can also take on a heavy load of work if you want to earn more or take on less work if you value the time more.

Managing your money:

- *Live on much less than you make.*

- *Develop at least a three-to-four-month buffer of money that can take you through lean months.*

- *Delay big ticket purchases until they don't eat into your buffer of money.*

- *Become a regular saver—pay yourself whenever you receive money.*

- *Don't buy things on credit—keep your monthly expenses as low as possible.*

Our consumer mentality is often to buy what we want on credit and worry about the bills tomorrow because *hey, I'm getting paid every other week right*? But the freelancer doesn't know when exactly they will be paid for work that they've finished. The phrase "feast or famine" had to have been invented for freelancers. Even though you might be finishing and shipping projects regularly, the checks seem to bunch up instead of trickle in over time. You can go a month or two without getting a check and that's the hardest part for a freelancer—waiting for those checks.

Here are some tips that might seem obvious but most of us struggle with this in the beginning:

1. Live on much less than you make.

2. Develop at least a three-to-four-month buffer of money that can take you through lean months.

3. Delay big ticket purchases until they don't eat into your buffer of money.

4. Become a regular saver—pay yourself whenever you receive money.

5. Don't buy things on credit—keep your monthly expenses as low as possible.

If you follow these five tips you will have much less stress over money and you'll be able to enjoy the times with less work instead of stressing about constant prospecting.

When should I turn down an assignment?

The truth is that early on, you will take projects that you'll wish you turned down after it's too late. This is inevitable because you have to be battle-tested in order to succeed in battle. It's okay to learn the hard way because it will help you develop your own criteria for taking assignments beyond the money. I'll give you a list of my red flags that might help you avoid the worst of the worst. Turn the job down if:

1. **The client cannot describe the image they want you to create or if the description seems like a big contradiction**

   A good client has thought through what they want or is willing to allow the illustrator to concept the image. A bad client doesn't know what they want, but wants to direct you anyway and the direction is confusing and often contradicting. Example: "I'd like you to illustrate a dynamic pose of a man standing erect and static." Dynamic and Static are opposites. Pick one—you can't have it both ways. This is a red flag and a sign that your client enjoys tormenting artists rather than creating a good product.

2. **Before the job starts, the client mentions anything about your payment being delayed for months because they have been having financial difficulties**

3. **The client simply cannot meet your bottom-line price**

4. **The client has a story or concept that goes against your moral compass**

5. **You cannot see yourself enjoying the work offered to you**

   Many times you'll get an offer to work on a project that isn't exciting or you think you'll end up hating. This is a huge red flag because even though you need the money, it's very difficult to do your best work when you hate what you're doing. Artists need to fall in love with their work in order to create art.

6. **You've booked too much work.**

   Obviously, this is a great problem to have. Even though you see the $$$, it's often better to turn work away than to overload yourself and turn in substandard work or late work. Let the client know that you really wanted to take their project on, but you didn't want to short change them by not giving their project enough attention. Ask them to keep you in mind when they have another project. I like doing this over the phone so that I can establish a connection that will help them remember me.

7. **You'll be working with a self-publishing author who has no idea how to get his/her book designed and published.**

8. **The client insists on using a "Work for Hire" contract and won't budge on allowing you to display the work on your website or social media after publication**

   (This isn't a done deal however—you might really need the money)

9. **The client won't budge on the deadline and you are confident you cannot finish the work on time**

   It's much better to be honest and preserve the relationship rather than taking on their project knowing you cannot turn it in on time.

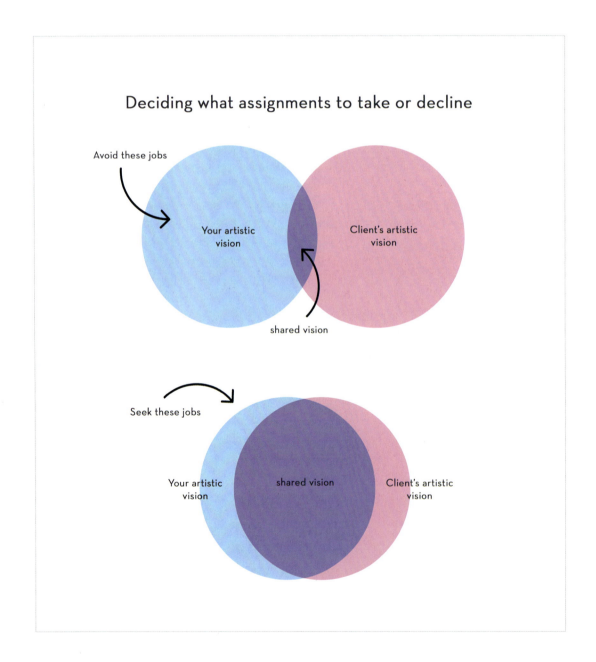

"I took my work ethic into the freelance illustration world and committed myself to constant improvement."

AFTERWORD

In the end, having a career in art is mostly determined by your sheer desire, passion, and commitment to having a career in art.

I was never the best in any of my art classes from high school through college. In fact, I was almost kicked out of my college illustration program and not allowed into the BFA program because my instructors felt that my work was at the bottom of my class. I was allowed in for one semester on probation to prove myself.

That was a stressful semester, as I always felt there was a target on my back. Perhaps that's exactly what I needed to have the motivation to work harder than most of my classmates. At the end of the semester, I had done well enough that they allowed me to finish my BFA.

I took my work ethic into the freelance illustration world and committed myself to constant improvement. Success comes from a combination of working hard—putting in long hours and being strategic in what you illustrate, the style in which you illustrate, and how you put your work in front of art buyers. Always remember that clients are looking for new and fresh work. If you create new and fresh work, meaning that your style feels new and original and unexpected, they *want* to find you. The question is CAN they find you? Are your social media accounts active and are you growing them? How's your website? Are you mailing your work out? If you are, and you aren't getting any work, it might mean that you haven't been at it long enough…or that quite simply, your work just isn't good and/or original enough yet.

AFTERWORD

Almost all successful veteran illustrators have one thing in common—they just never quit. They just put their heads down and worked...and worked...and worked.

"WHAT IS THE BIGGEST LESSON YOU'VE LEARNED AS A WORKING PROFESSIONAL ARTIST?"

I've asked twelve highly successful artists to answer this question and give their advice to up-and-coming artists.

Following are their answers...

Zac Retz

Zac Retz is a visual development artist working on animated movies and tv shows.

His main focus is color and design.

Clients include Sony, DreamWorks, Laika, Reel FX, Illumination, Alcon Entertainment and more.

Instagram:
www.instagram.com/zacretz

> "This may sound like a generic answer, but the most important lesson I have learned is to never stop learning and to be humble."

LESSONS FROM WORKING PROFESSIONAL ARTISTS

© Zac Retz, used with permission.

"What is the biggest lesson you've learned as a working professional artist?"

This may sound like a generic answer, but the most important lesson I have learned is to never stop learning and to be humble. I honestly believe this is the best thing an artist can do. Being a successful artist takes a ton of hard work, dedication, and sacrifice that a lot of people aren't willing to do.

It may mean a sacrifice in social life, video games, and/or hobbies. Say you spend a few years working really hard doing all the right things, taking the right classes, doing the studies and learning from the people around you and you finally get a job or you're able to make a living freelancing. A lot of people stop here. They get that first job with a decent salary and they stop learning. They do their work at work and that's it—no more art outside of work. When I got my first animation job, I could have stopped learning and pushing myself. I was getting other job offers and if I was comfortable, I could have just stayed as an average level/beginner vis dev artist. I could have stayed at the average pay level and just been comfortable. There is definitely nothing wrong with doing this. I actually am a little jealous of people who can relax and be content. I cannot relax though. I see so many very talented artists at work and online that motivate me to learn more.

So how do you learn more when you are already working a full day at work and may feel burned out at the end of the day? Of course, you will learn at work but I have found this is very minimal because when you are at work, most of the time you are expected to perform and deliver art constantly. You don't have the time to spend months learning about a new specific thing. You need to find a balance that works for you. Everyone is different, everyone needs different amounts of sleep or more recovery time.

People have told me that I'm a bit of a workaholic and I tend to get super invested in something and just focus on that one thing. I suggest getting up early, maybe start with one hour earlier for the first week, then push to two hours, then three or four. You may be surprised how much you can accomplish and how quickly your body adjusts to the new schedule. Me personally, I try to get at least six hours of sleep a night.

"You have to humble yourself and realize that there is always something to improve on as an artist. All the best artists I know are still taking classes and learning new things."

LESSONS FROM WORKING PROFESSIONAL ARTISTS

I get up at 4:00 am and spend about four hours in the morning studying, doing personal work, or freelance. Then I go to my full-time job. I do this work in the morning for a few reasons. First off, I love the feeling of being up before most of the world. It's still dark and I already feel a sense of accomplishment just for getting up. There's also a sense of urgency when you get up early. I know that in just a few hours I have to be at work so I don't let other things distract me. I am also able to focus better than if I were to stay up late. There's a quiet in the morning that's great for working and I don't feel burned out from a full day of work. This time in the morning makes for a great chunk of time to learn a new skill.

I also pack my own lunch every day. This way I save money and I'm able to have a bit of free time during my lunch break as well. I take this time to do a bit of personal work, or to read something about art. I have to be honest—I can't keep this schedule up year-round. Sometimes unavoidable things get in the way. Sometimes I teach a night class so I miss my bedtime of 10:00 pm or if I'm working out after work, I find my body needs an extra hour of sleep to help recover. This may mean I get up at 5:00 or 6:00 am the next day, but I always try to get back to my schedule as soon as possible.

A few ways to keep learning: *I like to take a class once in a while. Usually it will be an online class on some topic I want to improve on, or it will be some artists personal videos they make teaching some new 3D tools, or painting/drawing/designing techniques. Books are great too. I'm always looking for artist books that I can read and learn from. Observational painting and drawing is very important for learning too. I find that my color improves more in my work the more I go outside and paint.*

Always learning goes along with being humble. *You have to humble yourself and realize that there is always something to improve on as an artist. All the best artists I know are still taking classes and learning new things. That's why they are so good. Know that you can learn from everyone around you as well—co-workers and friends. This kind of dedication to your craft will lead you to great places. In just a few years you could double your salary, you could get new job offers that are your dream jobs, you will get more financial security. You will gain a level of respect among the artist community and from studios. It's really up to you and your goals as an artist.* ***Don't make excuses, make a schedule, stick to it and keep learning and growing to be the best artist you can be!*** ■

Denis Zilber

Instagram:
www.instagram.com/deniszilber

Denis Zilber is a freelance illustrator and visual storyteller with more than 8 years of professional experience.

He has worked with major magazines such as GQ, FHM, Maxim, Playboy, Blazer, The Pitch, Russian Life, National Geographic and newspapers as Yedioth and Maariv. He also works with animation studios like Hasbro Animation, Dreamworks, Nickelodeon, Rhythm and Hues, Eevolver. He has worked with publishing clients including: Penguin, Scholastic Books, Hotkey Books, Sterling Children's Books and Clubhouse Jr.

He teaches and gives lectures on illustration and storytelling traveling all over the world in many countries from Brazil to Mexico, the US, Portugal, Russia, Belarus and Israel.

> "Delivering the message is the key, nothing else. Storytelling is paramount."

LESSONS FROM WORKING PROFESSIONAL ARTISTS

© Denis Zilber, used with permission.

DENIS ZILBER – CONTINUED

"What is the biggest lesson you've learned as a working professional artist?"

At the very beginning of my illustration career, around fifteen years ago, I was desperately struggling to make a living out of illustration. While I can't say I had no flow of jobs coming in my direction, the vast majority of them were relatively low-budget ones. Literally speaking, I was making peanuts.

What made it all even worse was the fact that I was also constantly arguing with my clients, trying to defend my right to a certain artistic vision. I was really touchy about my art. Needless to say, such attitude didn't help me in maintaining any reasonable client base.

Back then I was in my late twenties, had a wife and bills to pay, so the whole situation was a bit of a nightmare for me. I was devastated, I didn't know what to think. Why didn't illustration work for me? Was it about my style? Or maybe my poor technique? I also thought maybe it was just my personal bad luck.

At some point, I even seriously considered a career change, presuming that probably character animation would prove to be slightly more profitable. So, I started to get into animation, and then after a year or so of studying animation, it suddenly struck me. **I realized that in animation, one of the most important principles is 'appeal.' The same rule applies to illustration as well, and just as animation should always be story driven, so should illustration.** Delivering the message is the key, nothing else. Not flawless technique or unique personal style, not even artistic self-expression. Though these are also important, storytelling is paramount.

It seems obvious and self-explanatory for some probably, but for me back then, it was an eye-opening revelation–almost of religious scale.

> "I stopped thinking of myself as a beautiful artistic snowflake entitled to special treatment, and started seeing myself as a professional–the one who gets the job done no matter what."

It changed everything. I reconsidered my career switch, and got back illustrating, but this time my main goal was solely focused on delivering a message.

I stopped thinking of myself as a beautiful artistic snowflake entitled to special treatment, and started seeing myself as a professional—the one who gets the job done no matter what. I also started seeing myself less of a fine artist and more of a storyteller.

Eventually this new approach paid off. My illustrations got better, more interesting, more appealing—I started receiving bigger gigs, my usual rates skyrocketed. **And, what is even more important, I started to enjoy my job—and my life more.**

That doesn't mean it's all unicorns and rainbows now. I still do encounter my good share of problems in my career, but at least I know what I am doing and **if anything goes sideways, I know how to make it right.** ■

> "Eventually this new approach paid off. My illustrations got better, more interesting, more appealing—I started receiving bigger gigs, my usual rates skyrocketed. And, what is even more important, I started to enjoy my job—and my life more."

Justin Gerard

Instagram:
www.instagram.com/justingerardillustration

Justin Gerard is an independent artist who has worked within the publishing and film industries providing illustrations for clients such as Disney, Dreamworks, Warner Brothers, Harper Collins, Penguin Books, and Random House. He has also worked in the game industry for Sony, Riot, Blizzard, Hasbro, Wizards of the Coast, Kabaam, Cryptozoic and Riotminds.

Justin's work has been regularly featured in art competitions such as Spectrum Fantastic Art, the Society of Illustrators Annuals and Expose.

He also contributes articles and tutorials for Artstation, ImagineFX and Muddycolors.

> "For me, turning a love of art into a successful business career was getting on a set schedule and sticking to it."

LESSONS FROM WORKING PROFESSIONAL ARTISTS

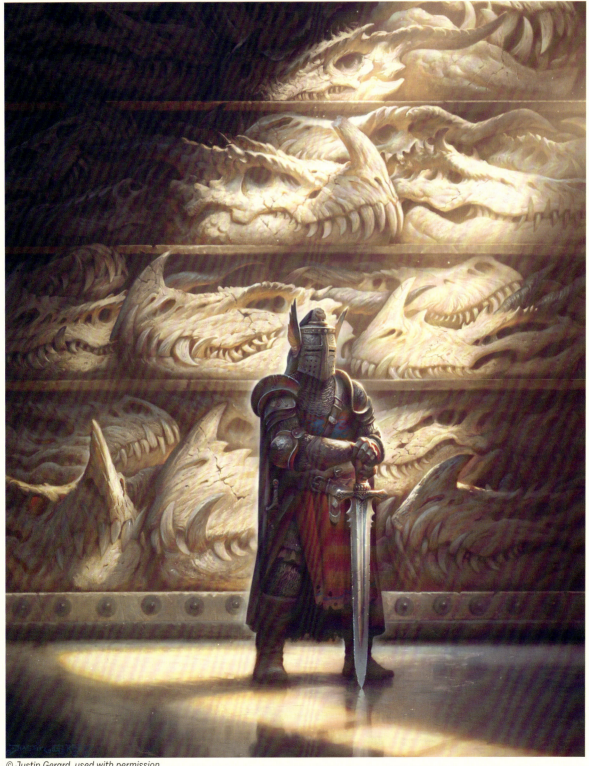

© Justin Gerard, used with permission.

JUSTIN GERARD – CONTINUED

"What is the biggest lesson you've learned as a working professional artist?"

For me the big key to turning a love of art into a successful business career was getting on a set schedule and sticking to it. As artists, we are generally curious about the world, open to new experiences, and shun conformity. A set schedule can feel unnatural to us, like you are "science-ing" all of the magic out of art.

But I found that a solid schedule was, in fact, one of the absolute best ways to ensure that I could continue having fun with my art as a lifelong career, and not just as a weekend hobby.

I began working on a set daily schedule after an old illustrator told me to "treat art like it's your job; eventually it will become your job."

> "I found that a solid schedule was, in fact, one of the absolute best ways to ensure that I could continue having fun with my art as a lifelong career, and not just as a weekend hobby."

"An old illustrator told me to *treat art like it's your job; eventually it will become your job.*"

And while I didn't work nine to five exactly, (more like 12:00 Noon to 4:00 AM), I did start putting in those consistent hours every single day.

My schedule now is to do emails and correspondence in the first part of the day, client work in the second part of the day, and then personal work with whatever time is left-over in the day.

And if I don't have any paying work? My job on that day is to practice, practice, practice—and to learn new skills and make new portfolio pieces until paying work eventually finds me.

I think it is important to acknowledge that we aren't perfect and we can always practice and improve. If I'm not getting good-paying work, it is probably because of gaps in my abilities, and I need to improve my work until I've overcome those gaps. ■

> "If I'm not getting good-paying work, it is probably because of gaps in my abilities, and I need to improve my work until I've overcome those gaps."

Piper Thibodeau

Piper Thibodeau is a freelance character designer and former DreamWorks TV character designer hailing from Quebec, Canada.

She has been creating a painting a day since 2012 for her "Daily Painting" series, which can be followed on her social media platforms.

Instagram:
www.instagram.com/piperdraws

"As a freelancer, try to keep your eggs in as many baskets as possible."

LESSONS FROM WORKING PROFESSIONAL ARTISTS

© Piper Thibodeau, used with permission.

PIPER THIBODEAU – CONTINUED

> "What is the biggest lesson you've learned as a working professional artist?"

A quick preface: I'm speaking as a freelance artist who works without an agent. My advice is less relevant to those who are interested in a full-time position, or those working with an artist representative.

Freelance artists working without an agent are often concerned about lack of work opportunities, which is not a common problem for those with a guaranteed influx of work.

As a freelancer, try to keep your eggs in as many baskets as possible. By that, I mean that it's important to seek work out from multiple different clients, as opposed to only one.

Working freelance with only one client is a risk that should not be understated—you're not a full-time employee, nor are you granted any union rights in most circumstances. I have had overwhelmingly positive experiences with my clients; however, there are risks to consider when doing any freelance work.

To name a few: A client's business could go bankrupt, there may be a crisis on their end that cuts a project short, you may receive late pay...

When you work with multiple clients, you're backing yourself up. *Even better, work from a variety of different subjects (board games, animation, children's book illustration... the list goes on.)*

> "Creating an income source from your own work is another useful tactic for staying afloat monetarily."

> "It's important to seek work out from multiple different clients, as opposed to only one."

WILL TERRY *What They Don't Teach in Art School*

LESSONS FROM WORKING PROFESSIONAL ARTISTS

You can't predict a dry spell in potential opportunities among the different industries. Perhaps you've been working doing animation all of your life, only to find studios shifting away from using freelancers. In such an event, having your foot in the door of doing children's illustrations can swoop you out of trouble.

Creating an income source from your own work is another useful tactic for staying afloat monetarily. *You can set some time aside to focus on your own artistic ventures while working freelance.*

Sell your own prints, books, show pitches etc. Working on your own artwork and posting it onto social media has the added benefit of being its own portfolio/ advertisement piece for potential clients. In my case, my Daily Painting project has helped me receive a steady stream of job offers. ■

> "Working freelance with only one client is a risk that should not be understated. When you work with multiple clients, you're backing yourself up."

177

Derek Laufman

Instagram:
www.instagram.com/ dereklaufman

Derek Laufman has been a professional artist for over eighteen years and resides in London, Ontario, Canada. He studied classical animation at Sheridan College which led to a 10-year career in game development.

For several years now, Derek has been a full-time freelance illustrator/designer working out of his home for Marvel, Warner Bros., Disney Publishing, Hasbro and Mattel. He is the designer of Marvel's Super Hero Adventure line as well as DC's Super Friends' new toddler-focused branding.

Derek also has recently created his first five-issue miniseries called RuinWorld published by BOOM! Studios in 2018.

> "Fan art *can* lead to professional work."

LESSONS FROM WORKING PROFESSIONAL ARTISTS

© Derek Laufman, used with permission.

DEREK LAUFMAN – CONTINUED

"What is the biggest lesson you've learned as a working professional artist?"

Fan art can lead to professional work.

There are people in the art community who tend to look down on fan art and write it off as stealing or copying—that it's a waste of time. There can be some truth to that, but if you are an artist who is able to put a unique spin on existing characters and make it your own, it can lead to some amazing opportunities.

I think it would be fair for me to say that most people who know my work discovered me through my fan art. I've always been a huge fan of pop culture and since I was a child, I would spend hours trying to draw the characters that I loved. It's always been a huge part of my life.

Later in life as a professional artist working in the game industry, I found myself working on art

> "If you are able to put a unique spin on existing characters and make it your own, it can lead to some amazing opportunities."

(for my clients/employers) that I wasn't allowed to share with the world due to NDA (non-disclosure agreement) contracts.

This led to me putting a focus on fan art, and I found that not only did I enjoy creating a unique take on my favorite characters, other people seemed to enjoy it as well.

"I enjoy creating a unique take on my favorite characters, other people seemed to enjoy it as well."

WILL TERRY *What They Don't Teach in Art School*

LESSONS FROM WORKING PROFESSIONAL ARTISTS

This led to my social media following growing at a much quicker pace, and soon I was becoming known for my fan art, above all else.

After about a year of turning my focus more towards fan art on social media, something happened that I had never planned on—both Marvel and a major toy company contacted me to work with them within a week of each other.

I hadn't contacted them. I never sent them a portfolio—but instead, they had discovered me through my fan art.

This led to me designing Marvel's Super Hero Adventures line for their toddler-aged products, which included, clothing, packaging designs and a series of children's books.

A year later, Warner Brothers contacted me to design a similar thing for their DC Comics toddler brand.

By putting my unique spin on familiar, existing characters, Art Directors were easily able to envision how my style would work for their established brands. **This is how creating fan art has led to a successful freelance career for me.** ■

> "By putting my unique spin on familiar, existing characters, Art Directors were easily able to envision how my style would work for their established brands."

Dan Santat

Visit him at:
dantat.com

Instagram:
www.instagram.com/dsantat

Dan Santat is a New York Times Best Selling author of numerous books which include the Caldecott Award-winning The Adventures of Beekle: The Unimaginary Friend, After the Fall, Are We There Yet? and Oh No! Or How My Science Project Destroyed the World, which won the Silver Medal from the Society of Illustrators.

He is also the creator of Disney's animated hit, The Replacements.

Dan lives in Southern California with his wife, two kids, and a menagerie of pets.

> "Understand that things take time, and that styles come and go."

LESSONS FROM WORKING PROFESSIONAL ARTISTS

I NEVER SHOULD HAVE BUILT A ROBOT FOR THE SCIENCE FAIR
科学博覧会のためにロボットを作るんじやなかった。

© Dan Santat, used with permission.

DAN SANTAT – CONTINUED

"What is the biggest lesson you've learned as a working professional artist?"

For many years, I've noticed that anyone who truly wants to make a living solely by freelancing can make it possible—either by working longer hours, cutting back on other expenses, or improving on their own abilities.

I've been freelancing for about 17 years now and one of the most useful lessons I've learned about surviving as an artist is **understanding that things take time and that styles come and go.**

When I started out in children's publishing, the majority of work I got was for funny picture books. One book would be published and then the next book I got would be another funny manuscript and I suddenly found myself type cast as "the funny picture book guy."

About ten years into my career, I wrote a more heartfelt and emotional story called The Adventures of Beekle, which was a metaphor about the birth of my son. As a result, it went on to win numerous awards but more importantly, **it showed everyone that I was capable of more than just creating funny art.**

Don't become a slave to style.

Style makes you applicable to a certain set of work. If you only do fantasy art, then you will only get fantasy art work. This is perfectly fine if that's your only desire, but the pool of work is also rather finite.

> "Style makes you applicable to a certain set of work. If you only do fantasy art, then you will only get fantasy art work."

"Be aware of your own limitations and create a more diverse set of work."

LESSONS FROM WORKING PROFESSIONAL ARTISTS

Meanwhile, there is a whole industry of other artistic means of expression that exist for you to make a living off of.

Don't be pigeonholed by your own stubbornness.

Be aware of your own limitations and create a more diverse set of work. *Art is a passion, but it's also a job, and if you want to excel then you have to cast a wide net.* ∎

"Art is a passion, but it's also a job, and if you want to excel then you have to cast a wide net."

Mary GrandPré

Instagram:
www.instagram.com/marygrandpre

Mary GrandPré has been a freelance illustrator for 30 years. She received her BFA degree from the Minneapolis College of Art and Design. There, she majored in illustration, with a secondary focus on graphic design.

As a freelance illustrator, her illustration projects range from advertising, editorial and packaging to concept painting and character design for animation studios. She has also illustrated several children's picture books—one of which, The Noisy Paint Box, won a Caldecott Honor. She also illustrated the well-known U.S. edition of the Harry Potter Books. Some of her clients include The New York Times, Harper Collins, Knopf, Crown Publishing, Random House, Scholastic, BBDO, Cincinnati Opera, Warner Bros, DreamWorks, Pacific Data Images, and Blue Sky Studios.

During her years of freelancing, Mary also taught illustration at the College of Visual Arts in St. Paul, MN and Children's Book Illustration at the Ringling College of Art and Design in Florida.

Currently, Mary lives in Sarasota, Florida with her family, and is developing her abstract painting practice.

LESSONS FROM WORKING PROFESSIONAL ARTISTS

© Mary GrandPré, used with permission.

MARY GRANDPRÉ – CONTINUED

> "What is the biggest lesson you've learned as a working professional artist?"

When I began my career as an illustrator, I had just graduated from the Minneapolis College of Art and Design.

I remember spending that first summer after my last year in school, re-doing many of the assignments I had done for my illustration classes. I wanted the "perfect" portfolio so that I could get out there and get my freelance illustration career started. After several years of waiting on tables, I was more than ready!

Little did I know, that one perfect portfolio would never come. **It was all going to be a path of learning.** That was the pre-computer age, when artists would schlep around huge portfolio cases from ad agencies to publishing houses and design firms. They would meet in person with potential clients.

It was a time when fax machines were a major way to get contracts and sketches signed off on, and when illustrations were created solely with art materials, not pixels.

A lot has changed for illustrators since then—not simply the way we make our art, but also how we communicate, and how we put ourselves and our work out into the world. The world has opened up more since then and it continues to do so more every day.

> "I have found that consistent exploration of new ways of working and thinking keeps my art moving forward."

Now, thousands of illustrators can easily be found with the click of a button—via their websites, Facebook, Instagram, etc. Technology has provided us with more efficient ways to market our work, and find more potential business opportunities. It should be so much easier, right?

Some things have gotten easier since those portfolio-schlepping days, but at least one thing remains the same: **Exploration, Discovery, Struggle, Breakthrough... Repeat.**

In my years of working as an illustrator and now as an abstract painter, I have found that consistent exploration of new ways of working and thinking keeps my art moving forward.

My art gets better and stays fresher when I ask myself "what if" and when I challenge myself with new ways of looking for a creative solution. Perhaps I try a new technique, or use a different color palette, or maybe it's about trying an unusual composition and an exaggerated perspective.

LESSONS FROM WORKING PROFESSIONAL ARTISTS

Being open to change and taking risks can be frustrating and it may not always produce good results at the end of the day. Sometimes those failed attempts can feel overwhelming. **That struggle, however, will propel you forward in your art practice.**

That is the only way to learn and grow, and that is how you find out what you are capable of. This process takes time, and it's an ongoing journey. But it's worth the effort, because your art is the absolute base of your business.

When you find what brings you the most happiness in your art making, you can focus on that, hone it, and go deeper with it—make it yours, authentic and unique. That is the kind of art that sells. It may not speak to everyone, but it will speak to some, loud and clear. So when it's time, you need to get it out there. With so many resources available today, it is indeed quite easy to do this.

Create a well-designed website, do research on the companies you would like to work for, compile contact information and create a mailing list. If possible, get feedback from potential clients, one on one. This is a great way to see how and where your work might fit in.

Building your practice with good people skills—along with resourceful marketing on top of a solid foundation of great artwork—will best ensure a successful art business. ■

"Some things have gotten easier since the portfolio-schlepping days, but at least one thing remains the same: **Exploration, Discovery, Struggle, Breakthrough... Repeat.**"

Tim Lee

Instagram:
www.instagram.com/rabbitrunstudios

Themes of music, Americana, pop-culture and bits of Southern Gothic often recur in Tim Lee's work, plus he is a self-professed fantasy/sci-fi geek, so that creeps in too. He enjoys creating these images on wood, paper, canvas, and screen prints. His recent gallery works have mostly been traditional media; but digital paintings are a big part of his work. Interested followers should keep an eye out for his booth at a variety of arts festivals in the Southeast.

Tim Lee earned a BFA from The Columbus College of Art & Design. He is currently exhibiting paintings in brick and mortar galleries in the U.S. and internationally.

He can also be found playing some "bluegrass-y" mandolin when he can find some "me" time. He currently lives in Pittsboro, North Carolina and is the co-owner/operator of ODDCO.

Lee also has a super-talented brother, Robert Lee, who, along with Mark McDevitt, owns and operates MethaneStudios.com

LESSONS FROM WORKING PROFESSIONAL ARTISTS

© Tim Lee, used with permission.

TIM LEE – CONTINUED

> "What is the biggest lesson you've learned as a working professional artist?"

The art business is a moving target and to come even close to hitting the target over the years, I've had to be willing to adapt but never accept mediocrity in my own artwork.

Everything changes over time in our line of work—design trends, potential clients, budgets, technology, advertising, delivery methods, artist tools, software, invoicing, and trending illustration styles.

The only thing that has remained constant for me has been the desperate need to personally grow as an illustrator.

I try to challenge myself each day to make my work better, experiment with new techniques.

> "I try to challenge myself each day to make my work better, experiment with new techniques."

I draw for myself, I paint for myself, and I pay attention to what is going on in the illustration industry so I can remain relevant in the art business.

It may be trite to say, but being your own worst critic may not be a bad thing, if it motivates you to grow. ■

> "It may be trite to say, but being your own worst critic may not be a bad thing, if it motivates you to grow."

LESSONS FROM WORKING PROFESSIONAL ARTISTS

"The only thing that has remained constant for me has been the desperate need to personally grow as an illustrator."

Lee White

Instagram:
www.instagram.com/leewhiteillo

Lee White spends his days breathing life into his imaginary world. He works primarily in watercolor, but likes to include all sorts of media, such as ink, colored pencil and collage.

He has illustrated a number of children's books, including Love, Santa and Emma and the Whale. His latest, Kate, Who Tamed the Wind, which was released in February 2018.

He has also done commercial work for various clients, including Marks & Spencer, Amazon, Laika, United Airlines, Verizon, Disney and National Geographic. He is represented by The Bright Agency based in New York and London.

When not busy with client projects, Lee creates his own personal work, which is shown at various galleries and art fairs throughout the year. Many of these images are included in a fancy coffee table book of his artwork, which came out in August 2017.

He also teaches all of his watercolor secrets through the Society of Visual Storytelling, an online art school for artists of all skill levels. >>

LESSONS FROM WORKING PROFESSIONAL ARTISTS

© Lee White, used with permission.

LEE WHITE — CONTINUED

"What is the biggest lesson you've learned as a working professional artist?"

Lee graduated with honors from Art Center College of Design in Pasadena, California, and earned his MFA in illustration, also with honors, from the University of Hartford in Connecticut.

He lives with his wife, little boy and two rambunctious kitties in Franklin, Tennessee.

The most important lesson I learned was that there are many outlets for selling the same piece of art.

For example, if I'm hired to make an illustration for a magazine, I start by getting the pay from that. Then, if I paint the assignment traditionally, I can sell that in a gallery. Then you can make prints from that image and sell those. Then you can license that image to other clients, etc.

Now I make images and then really look around and see what market they might appeal to. It has opened my eyes to thinking about business in a different way. It also increased my business tenfold and has exposed me to clients that I may not have thought about otherwise. ■

> "Now I make images and then really look around and see what market they might appeal to."

LESSONS FROM WORKING PROFESSIONAL ARTISTS

"It has opened my eyes to thinking about business in a different way. It also increased my business tenfold and has exposed me to clients that I may not have thought about otherwise."

Jed Henry

Instagram:
www.instagram.com/thejedhenry

Jed Henry is an illustrator, lifelong gamer, Japanophile, and all-around nerd.

He grew up copying art from game manuals, and years later, eventually got a degree in animation.

He now works full time on Japanese prints as one of the most prominent artists selling at comic conventions. He has all-but-written the book on how to "table" at comic conventions all over the U.S.

> "Keep pressing forward and sharing new experiences through your art!"

LESSONS FROM WORKING PROFESSIONAL ARTISTS

© Jed Henry, used with permission.

JED HENRY – CONTINUED

"What is the biggest lesson you've learned as a working professional artist?"

My advice to anyone wanting to become an illustrator is that they should try lots of different projects and applications for their art to see what sticks.

Often we create a project we like but the world doesn't respond to it the way we want them to, and we spend too much time trying to convince others of its value. Instead we need to try a variety of art genres and projects to satisfy our own interests, and let the world decide which ones it wants to support.

It's okay to keep our other interests as hobbies—and eventually you might find a home for those as well.

You may never find an audience for some of your work, but the key is to avoid becoming bitter with all the hard work you're doing.

In the end, you will have a variety of offerings, and your skill on all your projects will improve from your efforts—whether all of your work has a "following" or not.

Try not to be discouraged when you don't find support for some of your work. Keep pressing forward and sharing new experiences through your art!

> "It's okay to keep our other interests as hobbies—and eventually you might find a home for those as well."

"We need to try a variety of art genres and projects to satisfy our own interests, and let the world decide which ones it wants to support."

Jake Parker

Instagram:
www.instagram.com/jakeparker

Jake Parker is an illustrator, writer, and teacher based in Arizona.

Since 1999, he has worked on everything from animated films to comics to picture books.

Jake has lived in six states, working at the best studios with the most amazing and talented people in the country.

He started Inktober, a month-long prompt-based art challenge to create daily illustrations in October using ink.

He is a co-contributor to the 3 Point Perspective podcast and he also co-founded SVSLearn.com.

Currently he freelances out of his studio in Gilbert, Arizona.

> "You've created something a person can look at and know what you're all about."

LESSONS FROM WORKING PROFESSIONAL ARTISTS

© Jake Parker, used with permission.

"What is the biggest lesson you've learned as a working professional artist?"

I think every success I've had can be directly related to this one practice, which I have done since high school and continue to do to this day: Making finished products.

Every year I plan out a personal project that will result in an actual finished product that I then either give away or sell.

In high school it was little photocopied comics that I made for friends. In college I did the same, only they were drawn better. Since those early days I've gone on to make self-published books, t-shirts, sticker packs, prints, courses, and more.

When you're making something that you're either going to give to someone or sell, you are faced with a thousand questions that need an answer.

It requires you to give yourself a deadline, to learn how things are made, to learn new software, or learn how to work with others who can do things you can't do. It requires you to let go of perfection for the higher value of putting something finished out into the world.

When the thing you've been working on actually exists in the world, you now have a calling card.

> "When the thing you've been working on actually exists in the world, you now have a calling card."

"They see your vision; they understand your personality. Most importantly, they know you can deliver."

LESSONS FROM WORKING PROFESSIONAL ARTISTS

This product says you are capable of making things like THIS. You've created something a person can look at and know what you're all about. They see your vision; they understand your personality. **Most importantly, they know you can deliver.**

Every job I've landed, every person who's given me a chance, every big break that's come my way is directly connected to making something and putting it out into the world.

I'd write more, but I need to get back to finishing this book I'm working on. ■

"It requires you to let go of perfection for the higher value of putting something finished out into the world."

Mel Milton

Mel Milton is a prolific character artist who has successfully launched two crowdfunded anthology books of his artwork.

He is a former Disney interactive artist who left to pursue his dream of drawing and painting the best work he is capable of.

Mel often finds flaws in his work but his massive internet following shows his flawed "dooks" to be much more valuable than he would ever let on.

Instagram:
www.instagram.com/melmadedooks

> "You must learn the fundamentals of making great images."

LESSONS FROM WORKING PROFESSIONAL ARTISTS

© Mel Milton, used with permission.

MEL MILTON — CONTINUED

"What is the biggest lesson you've learned as a working professional artist?"

I am often approached by up and coming artists who want me to share with them the secrets to becoming a great artist.

I'm always flattered and humbled and I try to give them my best advice which they seem to often misunderstand.

I turn their questions around and ask them what they want to achieve with their art? What do they want to produce?

Often they will say that they want to make art like mine or that they want to learn the skills I have learned so they can draw like me. I help them understand that if they learn my techniques they will be copying me and not developing their own skills. **I try to help them learn that there is only one of them on this planet.**

You need to understand that you must learn the fundamentals of making great images. That includes developing great drawing, design, and rendering skills.

> "I turn their questions around and ask them what they want to achieve with their art? What do they want to produce?"

"As you develop your art, you need to develop your vision of what you want to share with the world."

WILL TERRY *What They Don't Teach in Art School*

LESSONS FROM WORKING PROFESSIONAL ARTISTS

As you develop your art, you need to develop your vision of what you want to share with the world. Each of you has a unique voice, and through the creation of hundreds and thousands of pieces of art, over time, your path will become clear...and then up-and-coming artists will ask you to share your secrets with them. ■

"Each of you has a unique voice, and through the creation of hundreds and thousands of pieces of art, over time, your path will become clear."

"There's nothing like finally being able to execute the vision of an image you had in your mind!"

NOTES

NOTES

NOTES

NOTES

NOTES

NOTES

"We only get a few chances to leave our mark in this world and I'm excited to share my experiences as a working artist and teacher."